ALSO BY STEPHEN A. MITCHELL

PROFESSIONAL BOOKS:

Relationality: From Attachment to Intersubjectivity (2000)

Influence and Autonomy in Psychoanalysis (1997)

Freud and Beyond (with Margaret Black) (1995)

Hope and Dread in Psychoanalysis (1993)

Relational Concepts in Psychoanalysis (1988)

Object Relations in Psychoanalytic Theory
(with Jay Greenberg) (1983)

EDITED BOOKS:

Relational Psychoanalysis: The Emergence of a Tradition
(with Lewis Aron) (1999)

Can Love Last?

*The Fate of Romance
over Time*

Psyche Revived by Eros' Kiss

Can Love Last?

The Fate of Romance over Time

———·———

STEPHEN A. MITCHELL

W. W. NORTON & COMPANY

New York • London

Frontispiece: Antonio Canova, *Psyche Revived by Eros' Kiss* (detail). The Louvre, Paris.
Photo: Erich Lessing/Art Resource, NY.

M. C. Escher, *Drawing Hands* © 2001 Cordon Art B.V.—Baarn—
Holland. All rights reserved.

M. C. Escher, *Möbius Strip I* © 2001 Cordon Art B.V.—Baarn—
Holland. All rights reserved.

M. C. Escher, *Relativity* © 2001 Cordon Art B.V.—Baarn—Holland.
All rights reserved.

"Fascination Begins in the Mouth" by Mary Gordon. Reprinted by permission of
Sterling Lord Literistic, Inc. Copyright by Mary Gordon.

Excerpt from "The Ballad of the Sad Café," *The Ballad of the Sad Café and Collected Short Stories* by Carson McCullers. Copyright 1936, 1941, 1942, 1950, ©
1955 by Carson McCullers. Reprinted by permission of Houghton Mifflin Company. All rights reserved.

From *The Collected Poems of Wallace Stevens* by Wallace Stevens, copyright
1954 by Wallace Stevens. Used by permission of Alfred A. Knopf, a division of
Random House, Inc.

"Fern Hill" by Dylan Thomas, from *The Poems of Dylan Thomas,* copyright ©
1945 by The Trustees for the Copyrights of Dylan Thomas. Reprinted by permission of New Directions Publishing Corp. and David Higham Associates.

For information about permission to reproduce selections from this book, write to Permissions,
W. W. Norton & Company, Inc., 500 Fifth Avenue, New York, NY 10110

The text of this book is composed in Simoncini Garamond
Manufacturing by The Maple-Vail Book Manufacturing Group
Book design by Charlotte Staub

Library of Congress Cataloging-in-Publication Data

Mitchell, Stephen A., 1946–
Can love last? : the fate of romance over time / by Stephen A. Mitchell.
p. cm.
Includes bibliographical references and index.
ISBN 0-393-04184-0
1. Man-woman relationships — Psychological aspects. 2. Love. I. Title.
HQ801 .M59 2002
306.7—dc21   2001044452

W. W. Norton & Company, Inc., 500 Fifth Avenue, New York, N.Y. 10110
www.wwnorton.com

W. W. Norton & Company Ltd., Castle House, 75/76 Wells Street, London W1T 3QT

1 2 3 4 5 6 7 8 9 0

FOR
*Margaret, Caitlin, and
Samantha*

Contents

Foreword

Margaret Black, C.S.W.

OUR WORLD IS FILLED with brilliant thinkers. We are regularly flooded with amazing information: details on our apparent potential to artificially replicate human intelligence, the intricacies of genetics, the increasing likelihood of producing a viable human clone. The issues that touch most directly on our everyday experience, however, remain somehow opaque, mysterious, conceptually documented yet experientially unresolved and unsatisfying. We have been granted one life to live. We want it to be fulfilling, meaningful. We want it to sustain love and passion. Many of us long for passion that will emerge and endure in a relationship with a particular important other. The questions seem easy enough to frame: What allows us to feel that our intimate relationships are passionate as well as meaningful? Can this kind of meaningful passion last over time? How can it survive, given the challenges we subject it to—living busy lives, dealing with everyday familiarity, raising children, growing older?

Our best thinkers seem to have little to offer us here. Despite his genius and astonishing productivity as the creator of psychoanalysis, Freud's formulations have not been particularly helpful, certainly not very optimistic. Within his conception of human psychology, sexual passion and enduring love have separate derivations, one primitive, one civilized, locking them in an inversely proportional relationship. A passionate sexual relationship with one's partner bodes poorly for tenderness and respect and vice versa. Psychoanalysis, which prides itself on reaching the deepest understanding of emotional life, seemed to have taken us to a conceptual dead end. Decades have passed since Freud lived and wrote, yet there has been astonishingly little new thinking in an area that affects us all so fundamentally.

Having lived with Stephen for nearly thirty years, having worked with him and raised a family, one of the qualities I always loved about him was his ecumenical approach to ideas. His kind of mind flourished in the contemporary postmodern intellectual climate, joyfully constructing and deconstructing, combining and recombining ideas gleaned from his extensive reading and clinical work.

Blessed with rigorous intellectual honesty, good thinking fascinated him—no matter what the discipline. He loved ideas, loved to play with them, to stretch them, to see how they held up on relentless probing, and, above all, to share them with others. He appreciated the thinking of others in a way that made their ideas seem like generous gifts for which he was deeply grateful. Accompanying him to a bookstore was like watching a kid in a candy store. We would inevitably leave, bags heavy with philosophy texts, poetry, a recently published novel, some obscure publication on physics that caught his attention, books on the mind, artificial intelligence, Buddhism, and, sometimes on psychoanalysis. There was a kind of implicit contest in our lives together: Would the prints I had purchased be successfully framed and hung on the wall before he claimed the wall space for another set of bookshelves? He listened to taped courses on the history of music while he exercised. He loved the fine presentation of ideas and read passages aloud to the family when he ran across something with a particularly fine turn of phrase or thought-provoking presentation.

Inheriting from his family of origin a healthy disdain for authoritarian structure, it quickly became clear that Stephen's thinking could not be constrained by rigidly held principles within psychoanalysis, no matter how distressing or disruptive his challenges were to the profession. Early in his own career, shortly after he had completed his training, he was among the first authors within the psychoanalytic tradition to openly and effectively challenge the then firmly held belief that homosexuality was fundamentally pathological (1978, 1981), an effort that eventually resulted in its removal from the official psychiatric nomenclature of pathology.

Stephen rather romped through the extensive literature in psychoanalysis which was, at the time, sharply segregated into competing theoretical traditions and heavily dominated by the classical Freudian approach, an approach that declared alternative positions to be "nonanalytic" and therefore marginal. In an effort to encourage more creative thinking in the field, he launched his own journal called *Psychoanalytic Dialogues*, employing what was at the time a revolutionary format of publishing the nonclassical marginalized voices within psychoanalysis as well as organizing respectful discussions among analysts of differing theoretical persuasions so that clinical approaches and theoretical formulations could be more thoughtfully and comparatively considered. He organized conferences, inviting representatives of diverse academic disciplines to consider a common problem in human experience.

Immersing himself in the divisions and controversies within psychoanalysis, Stephen became interested in what he felt were relatively unrecognized but potentially generative common threads running through positions ostensibly at odds with one another. With other like-minded colleagues, he began to redefine the psychoanalytic project, focusing not on the interpretation of sexual and aggressive strivings and symptom removal but on issues like the quality of life, the meaningfulness of personal experience, one's sense of self and a connectedness with others. In a culture where the analyst's knowledge and authority had defined the analytic process, Stephen's clinical approach, identified as "relational psychoanalysis," emphasized collaboration, open engagement between patient and analyst, empowering the patient's participation through thought-provoking questions rather than claiming privileged knowledge with declarative interpretations that presumed to reveal "what was really going on" in the patient's mind.

There were many issues that interested Stephen in his clinical work, but the question of how passionate connections stayed alive was always there—the frequent focus in his published clinical vignettes and a common topic of our discussions together.

While we both took great care to protect the identity and confidentiality of our patients, we enjoyed helping each other with clinical dilemmas and sharing new insights, mulling over the perplexing yet fascinating issues our clinical work raised for us. What was the underlying drama when a woman felt the "chemistry" was never right with the men she dated or when someone didn't know if he was "really in love" with another person? How could these personal stalemates be opened up, energized in the process of therapy, allowing the person to arrive at a truly meaningful answer? Was it an expression of our freer sexual mores—our greater interest in diversity—that married or committed partners so often had affairs? Or was this explanation an easy and comfortable cover for difficulties in becoming more intimate with a partner? Is there only one "right one"? Can one who isn't "right" become so? How much work should one put into a relationship? What constitutes productive work in a relationship—as opposed to a tedious kind of overanalyzing that avoids acknowledging the relationship is essentially not viable? Given that Stephen and I had been together for so many years, and cared very much about the quality of *our* relationship, we felt allied with our patients in their wanting help with these kinds of issues.

Stephen did not take on projects randomly—he was attracted to important areas where existing thinking seemed to him faulty or overly constricting. He had taken on issues like the structure of the psychoanalytic profession, the marginalization of homosexuals, the disenfranchised voices within psychoanalysis, the reconceptualization of psychoanalysis as a treatment; he wrote many books and an abundance of papers. Now for something really hard! He decided to think more systematically and write about love and passion in committed relationships. He wanted, in this project, to draw on the more contemporary and creative thinking within psychoanalysis, giving people greater access to contributions frequently missed in a culture that so readily and blindly equates psychoanalysis with antiquated Freudian formulations. Stephen also wanted to utilize contributions from outside psychoanalysis—contributions from philosophy, history, literature—in order to more deeply and productively engage the issues. He hoped to encourage a better connection between psychoanalysis and the larger world of ideas.

Having come to the conclusion that psychoanalysis had for too long unnecessarily and unhelpfully privileged its contributions to thinking-through problems, he decided that this book should not be directed toward the professional community of psychoanalysts but should be just for "people"—the more general educated public.

What can the reader expect of this book? Over the years, Stephen taught hundreds of students in his private study groups. His teaching within psychoanalysis was legendary: people joined his study groups and stayed in them for years as the content was never redundant, there was never a "party line" that defined his teaching. He sometimes spoke to me about a particularly frustrating class where students could only be critical of a reading that presented a point of view different from their own. He would describe his efforts to spark their curiosity, to interest them in considering the knotty problem the author was trying to unravel, to look at the issue from a new perspective, or to understand what a revolutionary contribution the particular author was making, if considered within the context of his or her orientation.

One of his students remembered the experience this way. "Listening to Stephen in our study group I've often imagined him as a weaver, always adding color and texture to a complex fabric, utilizing every fiber, every thread of thought." While Stephen certainly wanted to be respected as a thinker in his own right, he was not that interested in getting his students to agree with his particular thinking; he *was* interested in getting them to think.

As a reader of this book you are invited into a similar space. Parts of *Can Love Last?* are highly entertaining, the writing sometimes poetic, the stories of dilemmas and struggles personally recognizable. It is a decidedly thought-provoking book. It does not deliver its message on a silver platter to a passive reader awaiting enlightenment. As in his clinical work, Stephen assumes in his writing that the most powerful impact comes from the reader's deeply personal engagement in the process. He implicitly asks you to think things through with him, to puzzle over the paradoxical nature of the human experience of passionate connection, to pause and search your own thoughts and experience as you consider the clinical descriptions provided to explicate challenges to sustaining romance in committed relationships. Stephen invites you into a collaboration and in so doing acknowledges and supports your intelligent capacity to more capably take your life into your own hands.

Most important, I think you may find this book deeply moving in a personal sense. If you stay with it, you may find yourself pulled into nooks and crannies of your own experience and your own personal relationships—unfamiliar areas that you may never have really thought about before. You may find yourself not merely interested, but at times even perplexed, as though something within you had been opened like the door to a room you hadn't even known existed.

Can love last? Stephen is not asking a rhetorical question. Rather he is extending an invitation to all of us, an invitation to join him in rethinking some of the most profound and fundamental aspects of human experience in love relationships, allowing each of us to come away with our own personal answer.

—Margaret Black, C.S.W.
June 2001

The greatest weakness in contemporary thought seems to me to reside in the extravagant reverence for what we know compared with what we do not yet know.

—ANDRÉ BRETON

Oh as I was young and easy in the mercy of his means,
           Time held me green and dying
    Though I sang in my chains like the sea.

—DYLAN THOMAS

Introduction

SIGMUND FREUD ONCE ATTEMPTED to account for the widespread resistance to his prodigious contributions to Western culture by positioning his discovery of the unconscious as the third of three powerful blows to human narcissism. The first, the cosmological blow, was the Copernican revolution. If the earth orbits around the sun, rather than the sun around the earth, we are faced with the hard truth that human beings are not located at the physical center of the universe, not at its core, not at its navel. Rather, we ourselves revolve in orbit around another center. The second, the biological blow, was the Darwinian revolution. If we humans have evolved from other animal species, we are faced with the hard truth that human beings were not uniquely created. We were not instantaneously designed, of a piece, by divine inspiration, but rather emerged slowly, over vast periods of time, in fits and starts, as life responded to changing circumstances.

His discovery of the unconscious, Freud reasoned, was the third and most devastating assault, a psychological blow, to our estimation of our own importance. Prior to Freud's revelations, we humans, in our diminished state, one among an infinite variety of life forms, out at the periphery rather than at the center of things— we diminutive humans could at least claim self-governance. But, Freud demonstrated, the human being is not even "master in his own house": we do not even run our own minds. Mind is, according to Freud, a "hierarchy of superordinated and subordinated agencies, a labyrinth of impulses striving independently of one another toward action." Our conscious experience is merely the tip of an immense iceberg of unconscious mental processes that really shape, unbeknownst to us, silently, impenetrably, and inexorably, our motives, our values, our actions. This, Freud believed, was hard for us to accept.

I always thought Freud had this wrong. He was right about the immediate injury to the human sense of self-importance inflicted by each of these intellectual revolutions. But from his vantage point in history, Freud could not have imagined that the loss produced by each of these intellectual revolutions would be far outweighed by subsequent gains.

The fuller implications of our Copernican decentering emerged only centuries later. Not only are we not at the center of things, but our impressive sun is just one among billions of other suns, many of them much more impressive. Perhaps even more astounding, it was only with the acceptance of the work of Edwin Powell Hubble, years after Freud's death, that we humans began to realize that many of what we had taken to be other suns, perhaps other planetary solar systems, are actually other galaxies, and that these myriad galaxies, of which ours is only one, are catapulting away from one another at astounding speeds. In light of these developments, I have always felt our ancestors' sense of diminishment at Copernicus's discoveries, although very understandable at the time, to be almost quaint. What did we take ourselves to be, anyway? The center of everything? From our vantage point today, the loss of the overarching self-importance of our ancestors seems less consequential than the gains we have made in our understanding of the awesome, mind-rattling universe of which we are a part. Renouncing our claims to centrality has made it possible to regard ourselves as participants in something so extraordinary, so vast, that it would have been unimaginable to Copernicus, and even to Freud.

Similarly, even though it is nearly a century and a half since Darwin's remarkable genius enabled him to grasp the process of evolution and its basic mechanisms, we are still working out many of the implications of that jolting dislocation of humans from a wholly unique, hallowed position vis-à-vis other forms of life. At first, the immediate challenge seemed to be to theism itself. If we are not the product of an instantaneous creation, it was reasoned by believers and nonbelievers alike, then perhaps there is no creator at all. The loss of humankind's special status among other animals seemed inevitably linked with the loss of a plausible belief in the existence of the Divine itself. It was as if, to paraphrase Nietzsche, God and our elevated sense of importance died together. But in recent years more thoughtful religious thinkers (in contrast to the Creationists) have demonstrated that a belief in a divine design or divine will does not have to fall with evolutionary theory. Rather, theologians have come to appreciate the workings of the Divine in more complex, less simplistic terms than did our ancestors. And, for many nonreligious thinkers, a deeper relationship to nature and to life itself has emerged, across the varieties of environmentalism, as a contemporary secular religion. Regarding ourselves as one species among others in the infinite array of earthly life forms is generally no longer experienced as a diminution. Rather, an appreciation of our small place (and, perhaps, big responsibility) within the ecosphere has made it possible for many people to experience themselves as an inextricable part of something vast and beautiful—the panoply of life itself.

Decentered as we were within the universe, dislocated within nature, Freud's destabilization of our vision of the human mind as transparent to itself and ruled by conscious reason seemed yet another loss, difficult to bear. But like the Copernican and Darwinian revolutions, the Freudian revolution has also brought, over time, potential gifts for our always tenuous efforts to bolster our self-esteem. Here too, what we were defending turned out to be worth less than what now became available to us. Our conscious control over our minds is limited, we now realize. But we are not merely our conscious minds. We are also our unconscious processes, although not in quite the same way. What we are called upon to give up is a certain kind of hubris. What we gain is participation in something much richer and more complex than we ever took ourselves to be. We can no longer maintain our prerogatives as rulers over the small fiefdom of conscious rationality; gone forever is the view of ourselves as singular, transparent, self-generating, and self-controlling agents. We are multiplicitous, we have discovered, with areas of experience that are more or less opaque as well as areas of experience that are more or less transparent. Each of us has become a kind of variegated psychic community. Being a person seems now to be much more complicated and involving than ever before; it requires discovering ourselves as well as shaping ourselves, exploring ourselves as well as controlling ourselves.

Practicing psychoanalysis and psychotherapy, as I have done for almost thirty years, provides an interesting, in some respects unique, vantage point for observing and participating in people's struggle to understand just what and who they are. It is very difficult, I rediscover many times each day, for us to come to terms with the stark limitations on the kinds of control it is possible to maintain over our lives and ourselves. Yet we continue to insist, both consciously and unconsciously, that we have more control than we do over our feelings, our relationships, our fates. Freud's phrase for such fantasies, introduced nearly ninety years ago, was "omnipotence of thought," and we are just as committed to omnipotence today as were Freud's contemporaries. A conviction of being in control is central to our sense of safety; yet the imposition of illusory control chokes the richness out of life. Omnipotence degrades authentic experience into shallow manipulation. The more endangered we feel, the more control we seek; the more illusory are the controls we strive to maintain, the more vitality seeps out of our lives.

This book is about romance and its degradation. It is about romance, because I want to explore the struggle for vitality and meaning in the lives of those of us living at the cusp of the twentieth and twenty-first centuries. Vitality and meaning are not easy to come by, as evidenced by the endless succession of books, magazines, and television shows on self-help techniques, popular psychology, and popular spirituality. Modern life, at all points on the socioeconomic scale, is difficult, draining, and confusing.

What is it that imparts to life a sense of robustness? A quality of purpose and excitement? A feeling that one's life is worth not only living but also cultivating and savoring? Romance, I am suggesting, has a great deal to do with it.

There are many different forms of romance, including both romance in our relationship to ourselves and romance in relation to the world around us, what we take to be the "natural" as opposed to the humanly constructed world. Self-directed romance has recently been termed "narcissism," and many psychologists now consider it to be crucial to our sense of identity. And nature, the wilderness, is enormously alluring to many people in our time as something they want to get "back to." We will be touching on both of these forms of romance, but we will be primarily exploring romance as a form of loving others.

Aristotle claimed at the dawn of Western culture that we are social animals. But it is only in recent decades that we have come to appreciate just how thoroughly social we are. We are born with brains requiring extensive social interaction and language to complete their wiring. We become, inevitably and irreversibly, extraordinarily like the caregivers we require to nurture us through a lengthy dependency. And we spend our adult lives, to a considerable extent, with other people: actually present people with whom we live and interact; the ubiquitous virtual people of television, film, and print media; the past people who reside within us as memories and internal presences, inhabiting our subjective world even in solitude; and the generic people who have provided us with language and symbolic systems in which to think and organize experience. And because our lives are so much with people, the quality of our relationships with others is central to the emotional quality of our lives, the very lifefulness of our lives, the texture, the tonal quality, the verve.

The "romance" is a literary form appealing to emotion, the imagination, and ideals, and the Romantic movement was a revolution in consciousness as well as in the arts, a turn toward passion, the tragic, and personal meaning that has amounted to, according to Isaiah Berlin "the deepest and most lasting of all changes in the life of the West." We will be exploring the ways in which this pervasive historical shift in human experience comes alive in the individual lives of people in our time.

The term "romance," in its common, everyday usage, pertains to a particular feeling state and a mode of relating to another person, which generates emotions, stimulates imaginative play, and nurtures devotion to ideals. Romance emerges in relation to love, a particular sort of love in which there are powerful erotic currents. Romance is closer to "falling" in love than to being in love. Romance is also closely related to meaning, but not the ponderous kind or the important sort of meaning that can be generated by suffering and travail. The kind of meaning associated with romance is the feeling that life is worthwhile, that important events can and do happen within it. Yet, because of the inherent instability of romance, the tragic is often its counterpoint, making "the blues," with their expression of pathos and guilt, the quintessential romantic narrative.

People in our time seek romance to give their lives meaning. It often works—for a while. Romance can be captivating. It takes things over, adds verve, depth, and excitement about being alive. Yet what people in our time say about romance, across the spectrum from high culture to mass market magazines and tabloids, is that romance fades; it tends to be short-lived. Authentic romance is hard to find and even harder to maintain. It easily degrades into something else, much less captivating, much less enlivening, such as sober respect or purely sexual diversion, predictable companionship, or hatred, guilt, and self-pity.

What is it about romance that makes it so degradable? Most people, and most psychological experts, have opinions. Here are some of the most popular:

Romance fades because time and success are its enemies. Romance thrives on novelty, mystery, and danger; it is dispersed by familiarity. Enduring romance is therefore a contradiction in terms.

Romance fades because it is driven by sexuality, and sexuality is primitive in its very nature. In its raw form, lust is not a pretty thing and is difficult to reconcile with other features of romantic love, such as respect and admiration. So romance tends to degrade into either dispassionate friendship or purely sexual encounters.

Romance fades because it is inspired by idealization, and idealization is, by definition, illusory. We fall in love under the spell of fantasy; time is the enemy of romance because it brings reality and inevitable disillusionment. So romance tends to degrade into either sober, passionless respect or bitter disappointment.

Romance fades because it turns easily into hatred. There is a dark side to human psychology, and the delicacy of romance cannot long sustain itself against the power of innate aggression. Romance is like fireworks in the dark night, thrilling but inevitably transitory. We are lucky if we can simply get along.

Romance fades because nothing stays the same, especially people. We long for constancy in our relations with one another, but we inevitably betray one another miserably. Life itself is fundamentally tragic, and, ultimately, we all end up singing the blues, either about our own regrets (guilt) or about the failings of others (self-pity).

There is a ring of truth to each of these explanations, which is why they have such broad currency. However, their truths are only partial. We will be exploring each one, mining what is useful and reconfiguring partial insights into a fuller account. We will find again and again that it is not that romance itself has a tendency to become degraded, but that we expend considerable effort degrading it. And we are interested in degrading it for very good reasons.

I will be drawing on many sources, the most important of which are the lives of the people I have been privileged to know in my clinical work. Because of the need for confidentiality, these people are carefully disguised. There is nothing here that is simply made up, but often the cases are composites of work with several different patients with similar issues.

Despite popular misconceptions, contemporary psychoanalysis is very different from the "classical" psychoanalysis of the past. Traditional analysts tended to reverently apply Freud's pansexual imagination to all areas of human life in a way that was often reduction-istic, elitist, and authoritarian. But the heart of psychoanalysis, its most enduring contribution to Western culture, has been its com-mitment to the compassionate, collaborative study of the fine-grained texture of individual human lives, in all their complexity and intensity. Contemporary clinicians, particularly those identify-ing with the label Relational Psychoanalysis, have shed, along with the Victorian chaise longue, many other trappings of traditional psychoanalysis. What remains for contemporary analysts is the ana-lytic situation as an extraordinary window, not only into the inner world of each patient, but into the analyst's own heart as well.

In these pages, Freud is never taken as the last word, but he is sometimes taken as the *first* word—as the one who posed questions about fundamental aspects of human experience with which subse-quent analytic theorists, and all of us as individuals, continue to strug-gle. We thus will be trolling for ideas and understandings from psychoanalytic theory, both past and present, as well as from related areas like philosophy, history, linguistics, and especially literature. Harold Bloom has pointed out that while art mirrors or follows life, life mirrors or follows art as well: the great writers have invented forms of experience that were never possible before they wrote about them. This is nowhere more apparent than in what Shakespeare and Tolstoy have taught us about romance as a human potential.

The struggle to understand what is involved in the experiencing and sustaining of romance draws us into a thicket of issues and dialectics concerning fantasy and actuality, sameness and otherness, bodies and emotions, love and hate, the controlled and the uncon-trollable, pathos and guilt, safety and risk. Romance is a fragile and endangered condition. Romance seems like a simple, natural state. But romance and its place in our minds and lives are anything but simple.

1
Safety and Adventure

Being in love is like going outside
to see what kind of day it is.
—ROBERT CREELEY

BRETT, A MAN IN HIS EARLY THIRTIES, seeks psychotherapy because of difficulties in his relationships with women. Brett can't seem to find a woman with whom he can sustain his desire. He is physically attractive and has a position in the music business that enhances his appeal. Many women are interested in him, but he feels tortured by his inability to develop a relationship that works for him.

Brett generally begins relationships with a burst of passion and enthusiasm, only to find his interest waning. He starts to experience retarded ejaculation; his orgasms are more and more difficult to achieve; he sometimes loses his erection. He begins to wonder whether his lover is really the *right* woman for him. He then feels compelled to feign excitement and experiences the woman's intimate feelings as increasingly claustrophobic. He invariably finds himself longing for the freedom to date other women and soon falls in love with someone else, often someone who is not immediately available.

At one point Brett was involved with two women. Betty was around his age, of considerable intelligence and emotional maturity, and had begun to care deeply about him. Although Brett was excited about her at first, he soon encountered his usual problems with ejaculation. He felt a deep fondness for her, enjoyed her, thought he had even begun to love her, yet at times experienced Betty's feelings for him as cloying.

At around the same time, another woman, much younger, with whom he had once had a brief sexual encounter, reappeared in his life. Linda was a kind of music groupie, had metal studs in her tongue and clitoris, and beckoned him with the promise of sexual adventure. They went to bed.

In our sessions, a closer look at Brett's experiences with these two women proved somewhat surprising. On the surface, Betty seemed known, safe, and dull; Linda seemed strange, wild, and exciting. But analytic inquiry, as it often does, revealed an underlying inversion of what appeared on the surface. Despite her metallic accoutrements, Linda was detached during sex—intense but shallow. After having sex with her, Brett began to realize, he felt desperately lonely. Betty, in contrast, seemed to genuinely enjoy sex. She was quite adventurous and encouraged him to experiment. She seemed game for almost anything. But there was something about her very openness, Brett slowly discovered, that he found intimidating.

We began to focus on the times when Brett felt put off by Betty, feelings he previously would have tagged as indications that she was just not the right woman for him. These were always moments when he was in danger of feeling something deeply in her presence. He began to realize that it wasn't so much that he hated her, but that he hated her loving him, because her love opened up possibilities of his developing feelings for her that frightened him. It became apparent that Linda, the woman who seemed exciting, unknown, and adventurous actually offered experiences that were circumscribed, predictable, and emotionally shallow. Betty, the woman who seemed familiar and predictable actually offered experiences that were open-ended, unpredictable, emotionally limitless, and terrifying. Brett's difficulties with relationships derived from his inability to integrate desire and love. This is a very common problem.

Love and Desire

In a short, seldom-cited paper written in 1912, whose title is variably translated as "On the Universal Tendency to Debasement in the Sphere of Love" and "The Most Prevalent Form of Degradation in Erotic Life," Sigmund Freud asserted that "psychical impotence" was second only to anxiety as a form of neurotic distress in patients of his time. What he meant by psychical impotence was twofold. He was referring to impotence with psychological rather than physical causes. A man might be functionally potent in some circumstances but not in others: the problem was not in the equipment itself, but in his mind. But Freud was also referring to an impairment that did not necessarily manifest itself only in purely physical terms. In using "impotence" metaphorically, Freud was pointing to a *psycho*sexual inhibition, a constraint in the capacity to arrive at and sustain desire itself, a kind of psychological flaccidity. A man might be capable of performing the physical act, going through the motions, but without passion, without intense desire. And even though, as was the custom of his day, Freud often wrote as if men were the only subjects of interest, it is clear that in describing "psychical impotence" Freud was writing about a selective inhibition in the capacity to sustain desire with which both the men and the women of his time struggled.

Perhaps the most striking feature of Freud's clinical observation was that the condition most likely to interfere with complete potency, a full experience of desire, was love itself. Like Brett, Freud's patients could love, and they could desire, but they could not experience both love and desire with the same person at the same time. "Where they love, they have no desire," Freud noted; "where they desire, they cannot love."

The kind of epidemiological claim Freud was making about the prevalence of psychical impotence is always tricky to substantiate. But judging from my practice, reports from colleagues, both formal and informal, and recurrent themes in popular culture, Freud's observation seems to be just as true today. Many men and women of our time experience both deeply affectionate love and intensely passionate desire, but often not at the same time, not in relation to the same other person. Yet romance requires *both* love *and* desire; in fact, romance emerges in the tension generated by the simultaneity of love and desire. Love without desire can be tender, intimate, and secure, but love without desire lacks adventure, edge, the sense of risk that fuels romantic passion. Desire without love can be diverting and stimulating, but desire without love lacks the intensity and the sense of high stakes that deepen romantic passion.

Many men of our time struggle with a modified version of the Madonna/whore complex that was such a powerful motif for the Victorian gentlemen of Freud's day. Now it is often presented in terms not of the saintly Madonna versus the degenerate whore but of proper, more respectable women versus women who give themselves to sexual abandon, or of the familiar and dependable woman versus the anonymous and unknown woman who is ready for adventure. Many women of our time similarly struggle with a split between love for men they see as "nice" or "good," dependable and responsible, and desire for men they see as exciting, reckless, and at least a little bit dangerous.

We might imagine that the problem for Freud's contemporaries derived from residues of the negative, uneasy valence sexuality took on early in the Judeo-Christian and Platonic traditions that shaped our Western cultural sensibility. And we might expect the sexually "liberated" men and women of today, after the sexual revolution of the 1960s, to be able to love and desire, either separately or together, without internal conflict. But judging by the deluge of articles in popular magazines on putting spice back into relationships gone bland and romance into flagging marriages, whatever was troubling our ancestors in the early years of this century is still very much with us today. Given how much else has changed from Freud's day to ours, especially with regard to sexual mores and the presence of sexuality in the public domain, that is pretty astonishing.

Despite the emergence of sexuality from the Victorian shadows, despite the sexualization of advertising and the ubiquitousness of sexuality, people in our time seem to have as much trouble as people in Freud's time integrating love with sexual excitement, commitment with passion. There are quaint, anachronistic touches to Freud's 1912 sensibility. The genitals, Freud suggests, in a blend of Victorian prudery and species chauvinism, are an atavistic remnant from earlier evolutionary stages: "The genitals themselves have not taken part in the development of the human body in the direction of beauty, they have remained animal, thus love, too, has remained in essence just as animal as it ever was." We can only imagine Freud's shock at the emphasis on the genitals in contemporary aesthetics: in the spread of pornography, hard and soft, throughout both low and high culture, from Georgia O'Keeffe's flowers to phallic sports cars, and the cultural iconography of "hunks" and "babes." Yet despite all these changes, despite the extraordinary shift, which Freud's own work helped to effect, from sexuality lurking in the shadows to sexuality in our faces, for many men and women today, too, "Where they love, they have no desire; where they desire, they cannot love."

Stability and Adventure

In intellectual circles in these (post)modern days, it is hazardous to speculate about cross-cultural, universal features of human nature; everything is local, culturally specific, we are told. However, if I were forced to select an essential, wired-in aspect of human psychology, the sense of "home" would be high on my list. It is difficult for me to imagine a person—or a human culture, for that matter— who doesn't orient himself around some sense of home: my place, where I am from, where I belong, where I long to return. Home, wrote Robert Frost in "The Death of the Hired Man," "is where when you have to go there, they have to take you in."

It is no accident that the words "family" and "familiar" have the same roots. We seek continuity, sameness, as a way of grounding, anchoring ourselves, and each of us has our own particular way of going about establishing "home." The sense of place referred to in contemporary poetry reflects the way a geographical location, especially a place where one has spent childhood years, comes to penetrate one's mind with a deep sense of comfort for which there can be no substitute. There are people who feel at home only in the crowded bustle and electric intensity of New York City, or near the ocean-like expanse yet fresh-water feel of the Great Lakes, or dwarfed by the huge mountains Colorado, or gazing at a flat, endless Nebraska cornfield. There is a neurophysiology as well as a psychology to this experience: the sounds, smells, and images of our childhood and important passages of adulthood become wired into our brains in a way that is intrinsic to our sense of self-recognition, central to our psychological well-being.

Researchers who study infants have been observing this process in the subtle reciprocal influence and mutual adaptations that dominate the early months of life. The brain of the newborn, we now know, is incompletely formed; crucial neurological pathways governing basic biological rhythms of sleep/wakefulness, eating, and activity/quiescence are established through fits and misfits, complex and subtle negotiations, between the particular infant and the particular caregivers. The infant and the mother mutually shape each other to create a world into which the growing child will fit. The mother provides not just a supportive environment, not just a featureless container, but a *particular* supportive environment, with its own, distinct affective tones, its own sensory textures. We become our early significant others from the deep past. The profound feeling of connection and belonging that is evoked in the experience of "home," and in the presence of someone who comes from our home or with whom we have made a home, reflects a kind of matching, a pervasive resonance between what is inside us with what is outside us, between the past and the present, between what we were, what we are, and what we long to be.

There is also an archetypal dark side to the sense of home—a longing for escape, transcendence, the journey. The protagonist of Joseph Campbell's classic study of comparative mythology, *The Hero with a Thousand Faces,* who leaves home on his quest for manhood, wisdom, the Truth, has a thousand faces because he is portrayed in the mythologies of a thousand different cultures. We have to leave home to find ourselves, say mythic tales, including contemporary psychoanalytic tales of separation/individuation. Homes turn into prisons; enclosures become confinements; the lover who

was ardently courted and longed for becomes, in American collo-
quialisms, one's "old lady" or "old man," one's "hubby" or "ball-
and-chain."

The cross-cultural pervasiveness of the theme of home versus
adventure is reflected in the ways in which we live our daily lives.
On the one hand, we spend a great deal of time enclosing a familiar
space and constructing a home—staking our claim, securing stability, feathering our nest. On the other hand, we long for freedom
from the constraints which that very security places on our sense of
adventure and our thirst for novelty. It would be difficult to find
nest-builders so security-bound that they don't feel the lure of
being, to use Jack Kerouac's phrase, "on the road" again. And it
would be difficult to imagine wanderers so smitten with adventure
that they don't feel the tug of home.

There are often gender-based differences in the ways these
points of view are distributed and negotiated within couples, with
one partner, more often the woman, assuming the value of home
and the other partner, more often the man, assuming the value of
the freedom of the road. However, a closer look always reveals
both values in both partners. They are difficult to contain and sustain as a conflict within a single self, and so each of us is drawn
toward another who freely gives voice to what we also want but
are afraid to let ourselves know about or express. Men are hardly
less dependent than women on familiarity and security, but the
masculine sense of identity in contemporary culture is easily destabilized by dependency longings. Similarly, women are hardly less
adventurous than men, but they fear the impact of their adven-
turousness on the more traditional aspects of their feminine sense
of identity.

Thus there seems to be a fundamental contrast between the ordinary and the transcendent, safety and adventure, the familiar and

the novel, that runs throughout human experience. Scholars of comparative religion, such as Mircea Eliade, have written of the distinction between the profane and the sacred; theories of cognitive development, such as those of Jean Piaget, stress the dialectic between *assimilation* of new stimuli to established schemata and *accommodation* of those schemata to new stimuli. In psychoanalysis, most recently, Jay Greenberg has proposed a dual-instinct theory grounded in conflictual needs for safety and effectance. Each of these dichotomies points to two fundamental, conflictual human needs: on the one hand, a need for a grounding that feels completely known and predictable, a reliable anchoring, a framework, as Erich Fromm put it, for "orientation and devotion"; on the other hand, a longing to break out of established and familiar patterns, to step over boundaries, to encounter something unpredictable, awe-inspiring, or uncanny. Romantic passion emerges from the convergence of these two currents.

Love and Romance: An Unstable Marriage

Although there are accounts of instances of romantic passion throughout antiquity, some historians date the emergence of romantic love as a universal potential and a literary genre to the institution of "courtly love" in the late middle ages, coincident with the beginnings of what would develop into the modern notion of the personal self. Whereas the classical and medieval epic portrayed life as a test of endurance oriented toward the hereafter, the early Renaissance romance began to portray life in terms of a personal quest. There is something at stake for the individual in leaving the security of the familial and the familiar, in overstepping established boundaries into the unknown. Romantic love became almost paradigmatic of the transcendent experience; it was at once both erotic and sacred.

The lady loved by the knight, like Beatrice for Dante, might be virtually unknown, glimpsed only from afar. It was her very status as beyond the ordinary that made her extraordinary and opened up the possibility of transcending the boundaries of the familiar. In romantic passion, the lover attributes illusory (fantasied) value to the beloved, who becomes the embodiment of ideals of beauty, power, perfection.

Courtly love developed at a time when marriage was an economic and political contract arranged by families. Romance, by contrast, was located outside marriage, in a world of feelings that appeared spontaneously without arrangement. Any romantic love worthy of its name was enduring, not because of obligation or commitment, but as reflective of the depth of passion and devotion of the lovers. And marriage tended to be regarded as usefully, necessarily devoid of passion, to keep it spiritually pure and safe from baser instincts.

However, by the seventeenth century in both Europe and America, the polar concepts of marriage and love began to converge. Marriage was understood increasingly as a passionate bond, and the partners in arranged marriages were expected to grow to love each other. Marriage should lead to romance, it was now believed. By the nineteenth century, as arranged marriages became less the norm, the sequence had become reversed: it was not that marriage led to erotic passion, but that erotic passion and adventure led to marital love. Love had become more fully sexualized, and romance was now regarded as the initial spark that would, over time, become modulated into a stable basis for marriage and childrearing. By the early twentieth century, as the popular song suggested, "Love and marriage, love and marriage, go together like a horse and carriage."

Passion and commitment reflect very different values, both of which have deep roots in the American psyche. In *Habits of the Heart,* one of the most thoughtful sociological studies of the American experience over the past several decades, Robert Bellah and his co-authors explored the complicated, often paradoxical tension between the ideals of freedom and obligation, between individualism and commitment, that so powerfully shape the American experience. "Americans are, then, torn between love as an expression of spontaneous inner freedom, a deeply personal, but necessarily somewhat arbitrary, choice, and the image of love as a firmly planted, permanent commitment, embodying obligations that transcend the immediate feelings or wishes of the partners in a love relationship."

The alliance between passion and commitment, between love and marriage, has always been unstable. Traditional psychoanalytic theorizing, for example, has generally taken a dim view of the romantic, idealizing dimension of loving, understanding it as fundamentally regressive and defensive. Romantic love has been regarded as, at best, a brief prelude to more stable, ambivalent love; once reality intervenes and one gets to know the other as he or she "really" is, the idealization that fuels the illusions of romantic love is no longer possible. Romantic desire might point the way, but many experts considered it a dangerous and unstable basis for shaping a life. Love and marriage may go together like a horse and carriage, but it is crucial that the horse of passion quickly be tethered by the weight of the carriage of respectability to prevent runaways.

The sexual revolution of the 1960s defied that caution. As the importance of sexual pleasure and gratification became a central value, premarital sex became more widely accepted as a proving ground for love and a precondition for commitment. Expectations for the amount of sexual gratification a marriage could and should provide over time were greatly heightened, and the rising divorce rate clearly reflected the frequency of disillusionment in marital relationships measured by this new criterion. Through the sexual revolution, in both its more dramatic and also its subtler impact on our culture, sexual satisfaction became a kind of inalienable birthright for both men and women, an ultimate value; the viability of relationships was often measured against that single standard.

These developments were reflected in the Gay Liberation movement as well. The Puritan-based theological and moral critique of homosexuality has always been a background feature of American culture. But in the mid-twentieth century psychiatry and psychoanalysis turned this condemnation into a full-scale assault, branding homosexuality as sin and disease. Renunciation, it was argued, was crucial. Partly in response to this pressure, the gay identity that was forged in the 1960s was shaped around the claim that choice is impossible. As Gay Liberation gained steam, it took as fundamental principles that one's sexual orientation is a reflection of one's deepest self, that changing one's sexual orientation is impossible, and that the only choice is between self-expression and self-suffocation.

This identity principle was consistent with the more general conviction of the times: sexuality is central to self, and happiness in life depends greatly on its expression and gratification. Even though the AIDS epidemic and the neofundamentalist backlash have put the brakes on the sexual revolution over the past two decades, the search for ideal sexual satisfaction remains. Disease made sex with multiple partners too adventurous and risky for many, and stable, familiar relationships became less expendable. Nevertheless, most of us still believe that our self is reflected and expressed in our sexuality, a belief that makes the pursuit of romance, within or outside long-standing relationships, a popular life's work.

Security and Its Illusions

The customary tale of psychic impotence, in both popular and psychoanalytic literature, portrays the thrill of illicit and dangerous sexuality as mysterious and requiring explanation. Why does the woman who loves her steady and dependable husband feel sexual excitement only in transient situations with threatening men? Why does the man who is grateful to his devoted wife perpetually find someone else's wife fascinating?

When psychoanalysts try to explain something they do not understand, they often reduce it to a childhood precursor. Thus danger, the illicit, the crossing of boundaries, the lust for adventure—these have all generally been understood as re-creations of childhood, forbidden oedipal longings. There is a conflict between the drabness of the known and familiar and the excitement of the unknown, which provides room for childhood oedipal fantasies to emerge. The obvious solution in this traditional account is renunciation: the rationality of adult maturity must triumph over the illusions of infantile fantasy. The ill-fated lover is enjoined to grow up and rededicate himself to the drab, predictable familiarity of his ordinary life!

But I have found it useful in these kinds of clinical situations to reverse the question and ask, rather: How is it that in his or her primary relationship this man or woman manages to feel so safe? With such patients, it is as if the available is assumed to be completely known, always accessible, wholly predictable. Safety is presumed. But in exploring in detail the textures of such established relationships, I have invariably discovered that the sense of safety is not a given but a construction, the familiarity not based on deep mutual knowledge but on collusive contrivance, the predictability not an actuality but an elaborate fantasy. So often, in long-standing relationships that break apart, one or both partners discover with a shock that the assumptions they made about the other's experience, the very convictions that made the other both safe and dull, were inventions, often collusively agreed upon. The husband really was not so dependable; the wife was really not so devoted. They often discover that their dull "partner" has had all sorts of secrets, very private thoughts and feelings, and, perhaps, a clandestine relationship to express them in. "She is not the person I thought she was," is the lament of the betrayed. Precisely.

How knowable and predictable *is* another person? How knowable and predictable are we to ourselves? Psychologists and philosophers have traditionally portrayed the self as very knowable indeed: the self is built of stable and predictable structures; there is a continuous, core self; at the heart of the self is a singular kernel that, if safety is presumed, seeks validation. But there are newer theoretical currents that portray the self as much more inaccessible, decentered, fluid, and discontinuous.

From this newer perspective, it is not adventure and danger that need explaining, but claims to predictability and safety. The longing for the inaccessible and the sense of "possession" of the known are Janus-faced illusions that function to contain risk and uncertainty. To long for the unavailable object is to segregate desire into a domain in which its fate is predetermined. Unrequited love is painful but safe. Conversely, the sense of security, possession, ownership that often attends long-term relationships is partially a contrivance based on fantasies of permanence.

There is a powerful motive at work in long-term relationships to establish security, a predictability over the unpredictable, a knowingness over the unknown. The essayist Adam Phillips has noted:

> Knowing people—or certain kinds of knowledge about people— can be counter-erotic; the unconscious intention of certain forms of familiarity is to kill desire. It is not simply that elusiveness, or jealousy, sustains desire, but that certain ways of knowing people diminish their interest for us; and that this may be their abiding wish. So we have to watch out for the ways people invite us—or allow us— to know them; and also alert ourselves to the possibility that knowing may be too tendentious, too canny, a model for loving.

Phillips is pointing to certain forms of knowing, coercive forms, which strive to fix the fluidity and multiplicity of the other into a predictable pattern. This form of knowing kills romantic passion, and this is a kind of knowing that is very prevalent in long-term relationships. It has strong appeal. It seems to be security-enhancing (like all security operations, only in the short run). But it is coercive and illusory.

Habituation, we are told, kills desire. But how does a lover become a habit? Habits are very useful for mechanical tasks, like washing dishes and brushing one's teeth. But habits are deadly to relationships. We probably all make habits, to some degree, out of those we love—but think about how unfair and infuriating it feels, how reductive of one's complexity and humanity, to have *oneself* made into a habit! I am suggesting that the habituation that often, perhaps usually, dulls romantic love is not intrinsic to the nature of love itself but is a protective degradation, a defense against the vulnerability inherent in romantic love. It is also a consequence of love's developmental history.

Attachment and the Coziness of Love

One of the things good parents provide for their children is a partially illusory, elaborately constructed atmosphere of safety, to allow for the establishment of "secure attachment." Good-enough parents, to use D.W. Winnicott's term, do not talk with young children about their own terrors, worries, and doubts. They construct a sense of buffered permanence, in which the child can discover and explore, without any impinging vigilance, her own mind, her creativity, her joy in living. The terrible destructiveness of child abuse lies not just in the trauma of what happens but also in the tragic loss of what is not provided—a protected space for psychological growth.

It is crucial that the child does not become aware of how labor-intensive that protected space is, of the enormous amount of parental activity going on behind the scenes. But as adults we gradually learn how managed was that cocoon-like space our caregivers were able to provide. Thus the kind of certainty and control inherent in the secure attachment that children feel for their parents is partially an illusion, and it is crucial that the spell not be suddenly broken. That is why the precipitous loss of attachment figures is so disastrous for children.

Even under the best of circumstances, the control parents struggle to exert over the environments they offer their children is itself at least partially illusory. Parents, like all people, have only limited access to and control over their own feelings. Therefore, children are deeply affected by many features of their early interpersonal environment of which parents themselves may or may not be aware. The parents' secrets are often a palpable presence in the household, even if, or sometimes especially if, they remain unarticulated. And out-of-awareness features of the parents' experience, unconscious conflicts and disclaimed passions, are often picked up by children as alluring, forbidden, and mysterious. The very features that parents segregate out of the secure home base they are trying to provide for the child often become the most intriguing, exciting features of the child's experience and thus are imprinted into the child's desire.

We learn to love in the context of the contrived and necessary safety of early childhood, and love seeks, perpetually, a kind of safety that screens out the unknown, the fantastic, the dangerous. The great irony inherent in our efforts to make love safer is that those efforts always make it more dangerous. One of the motives for monogamous commitments is always, surely, the effort to make the relationship more secure, a hedge against the vulnerabilities and risks of love. Yet, since respectable monogamous commitment in our times tends to be reciprocal, the selection of only one partner for love dramatically increases one's dependency upon that partner, making love more dangerous and efforts to guarantee that love even more compelling. So we pretend to ourselves that we have, somehow, minimized our risks and guaranteed our safety—thereby undermining the preconditions of desire, which requires robust imagination to breathe and thrive.

Susan, a woman in her mid-forties, seeks psychoanalytic treatment because she is confused about some of the choices she has made and afraid that her life is in danger of becoming a sociological cliché. Her childhood was quite impoverished, both materially and interpersonally. What shreds of security she had were imposed by her mother through a religious piety that felt contrived but sustaining. Susan had a very bumpy adolescence and early adulthood but managed to use her considerable intelligence and creativity to fashion a satisfying, if dull, life for herself. She shared with her husband and children a family life that felt quite rich and meaningful to her. Yet two years before entering treatment she began an affair with a younger man, which she pursued with a recklessness that both excited and frightened her. Was this a midlife crisis? Should she renounce the excitement of the affair and settle maturely for a comfortable domestic existence? Or should she abandon familiarity and conventionality and seek a more authentic if dangerous life with her lover? There was something about the very banality of the choice, as if right out of a made-for-TV movie, that both depressed and paralyzed her.

I was often struck by the way Susan systematically undersold herself. She was a woman of great talents and appeal, but her sense of herself was always of someone living on the edge of collapse. As we came to understand how her marriage was put together, it became clear that it was partly marriage, partly potential day hospital. Her husband was a caring, somewhat doting man who conveyed to her a perpetual availability and responsiveness. She complained bitterly about the anti-erotic impact of this doting, but the more closely we explored the arrangements of their lives, the clearer it became that she counted on it and in some sense insisted on it. She believed that the dullness of her marriage and the excitement of her affair derived from properties of the two men themselves. I pointed out ways in which she insisted on her marriage remaining dull and predictable and segregated her risk-taking into the other relationship. I suggested that, despite her successes and durability, she was always preparing herself for a collapse and required her husband to be dull and dependable to take care of her. Both relationships began to change as she became aware of the ways she orchestrated excitement in the one and dreary predictability in the other.

She was surprised to discover how inhibited she was in her interactions with her husband and began talking to him about wanting to open things up between them. He responded, at first somewhat cautiously, and she reported one Monday that they had had an uncharacteristically romantic weekend away. He had even responded to her interest in moderately kinky sex in a way that had been much more exciting for her. "It was a lovely weekend," she said, "very cozy."

I was interested in her use of the word "cozy." Cozy was a word she had used in relation to her husband when he was padding around in slippers serving her coffee. Cozy was not a word she would ever use in relation to her lover. "Cozy" seemed an odd way to characterize the break in protocol that had taken place over the weekend. Susan and I came to feel that the word choice here was an important part of the way she processed her experience to maintain herself as a sociological cliché, to refurbish a familiarity and predictability that she felt she might desperately need someday, against which she needed to continually rebel to find something more authentic and alive in herself.

The need to feel one knows both oneself and another person, the need for a wholly secure attachment, is powerful both for children and for adults. But in human relationships safety and predictability are difficult to come by. We endlessly strive to reestablish that illusory sense of permanence and predictability. When patients complain of dead and lifeless marriages, it is often possible to show them how precious the deadness is to them, how carefully maintained and insisted upon, how the very mechanical, totally predictable quality of lovemaking serves as a bulwark against the dread of surprise and unpredictability. Thus "secure attachment" is not a terribly useful model of mutual, adult romantic love, except in its fantasy, illusory, security-bolstering dimensions. Love, by its very nature, is *not* secure; we keep wanting to make it so.

The Illusion of Safety and the Segregation of Imagination

Einstein's physics shows us that motion cannot be gauged in absolute terms but only in relative ones. If I am sitting still on a trans-Atlantic airplane, I am in motion in relation to the surface of the earth and at rest in relation to my fellow passengers. Psychologically, too, rest and motion are relative. They depend a great deal on where one is and on where one wants to be.

We long to view our emotional lives as secure and familiar, at rest; and we long to move, to transcend the boundaries of our psychic enclosures. But how safe and static is home? How secure are our enclosures? Is safety realistic? Is adventure a fantasy?

If we assume there is a fundamental reality to our sense of security and stability, then it is motion, the gap, transience which creates space for imagination, making desire possible. But if we assume that human experience is, by its very nature, in flux, that perpetual motion and change are inherent to our nature, then it is home and security that are generated through an act of imagination. And motion and transience become the fundamental ground of our experience, a fluidity that is often difficult to bear. In this inversion, flux and adventure become realities, and security and safety appear fantastic. Ultimately, both our sense of home and our sense of quest entail, in some measure, an act of imagination.

Our psychic life and loves oscillate back and forth between aloneness and connection. Both can be frightening; both are risky. The dangers inherent in each can be circumvented through contrivance and fantasy. Thus the unconscious contract that parallels many legal marriage contracts is an agreement to pretend to be permanently, unalterably, impossibly bound—an agreement that creates the necessity for a carefully guarded, perpetually measured distance. Jacques Lacan, the influential French psychoanalyst, seems never to have grasped the possibility of a genuine relatedness, but he captured vividly the mirages of degraded romance in the service of illusory security: "Love," he noted, "is giving something you don't have to someone you don't know."

It is common for couples with a vibrant sexual life to fear marriage. That fear is not wholly ungrounded. Of course, it is not marriage itself that kills desire, but the way in which marriage can be constructed. We long for certainty and absolute safety to protect our love. And the common marriage vow—" 'til death do us part"—seems to promise reassurance precisely along these lines. Before marriage, couples often experience themselves as free, childlike, adventurous, and spontaneous. In marriage, they seek stability and permanence. In marriage they may come to identify themselves and each other as "adults" now, like their own mothers and fathers—as static institutions. And they attribute the deadening that comes with stasis to the institution of marriage itself, rather than to their own conflictual longings for certainty and permanence with which they construct the meaning of their marriage for themselves.

Total safety, predictability, and oneness, permanently established, quickly become stultifying. William Blake, the visionary Romantic poet, was among the first to discern that the secret hero of Milton's *Paradise Lost* was not God but Satan. Because it is illusory and contrived, permanent safety stifles vitality and generates expressions of exuberant defiance. It is striking how frequently members of separating couples reclaim and explore their sexuality under the banner of "giving myself the adolescence I never had." In reality, virtually no one actually had the adolescence they wish they'd had, built around a vision of free sexual expression, unconstrained by concerns for security or convention. This is why it is difficult for many people to find a place for adolescent versions of self in long-term relationships founded upon collusive contracts of illusory safety. Sexuality is perfectly designed for rebellion against such contracts, precisely because sexual response can be neither willed nor willfully controlled. Sexual arousal is unruly and unpredictable; it entails vulnerability and risk; it gives the lie to illusions of safety and control.

Fantasies of sex with someone unavailable or inaccessible, fantasies of sex with the mysterious stranger, are extremely compelling. Their allure derives not simply from the opportunity they provide for exploring the forbidden and precarious, but from the opportunity they provide for fantasizing about the forbidden and precarious in a safer venue than our actual relationships, in which we are loath to allow ourselves to become destabilized.

The Beast on a Leash

Oscar entered treatment because a growing sense of dissatisfaction had nearly led him to end a relationship of many years. This relationship had been very gratifying to him in many ways, but Oscar had never agreed to marry his girlfriend, mostly because he felt she was quite constricted sexually. He continually felt driven to flirt with other women and was adept enough at it that he always had several relationships that he could easily have sexually consummated. Until he became infatuated with one of these other women, who he felt was clearly less desirable than his girlfriend in many other respects, these dalliances gave him the excitement he felt he needed because of her inhibitions.

Not just Oscar's behavior but also his speech was constricted with his girlfriend, who, he was quite certain, regarded him as "bestial"; he did not feel he could share with her his sexual thoughts and fantasies, his past sexual experiences, because, he was sure, she would take these as evidence of wavering in his commitment to her.

Over the course of our work, we came to understand the ways in which Oscar perpetually conveyed to his girlfriend the idea that his sexuality was a great danger to their relationship. There was something terribly important to him about experiencing himself and being regarded by her as a wild, dangerous, pansexual creature who, if not for her control over him, would be ravishing every woman in the neighborhood. There was something centrally important to him, I suggested, about experiencing himself not just as a beast but as a "beast on a leash." The leash was at least as important as the bestiality, and he was adept at luring his girlfriend into exerting an external control on what he liked to think of as his sexual voraciousness. In terms of actual sexual encounters, he was the most loyal of lovers, but, like the juggler who keeps many plates spinning concurrently, he led an exhausting life.

Was this essentially a conflict of different sexual sensibilities? I think not. We came to think of this issue in broader terms after one session which Oscar began by reflecting on his difficulty in knowing where to begin. There were so many things he wanted to talk about, to consider; he pictured them laid out before him like food on a smorgasbord. He felt hesitant about choosing a starting point, for fear of losing the other topics. I was struck by this image and asked for his associations to smorgasbords. He had grown up in a working-class neighborhood of a big city, with few nice restaurants. At some point during his childhood a Swedish restaurant opened and became an instant hit. The opportunity to consume as much as one wanted for a fixed price was irresistible. He and his family frequented this restaurant, but they saw themselves as superior to the others there in terms of social class and moral refinement. An important part of this dining experience for them was to watch with amusement as their fellow customers returned, again and again, to heap their plates full of food, while they themselves acted with great restraint. If their neighbors indulged in oral greediness, theirs was an orgy of righteousness.

Oscar and I came to appreciate the centrality of the theme of restraint in the way he conducted his life. One of the most important functions of the relationship with his girlfriend was that it allowed him to demonstrate his fidelity, despite continual frustration and perpetual, intense temptation. This righteousness established and preserved his sense of his own goodness and lovability and, therefore, gave him an illusion of absolute security.

Constructing Security and Desire

Love and desire generate the arc of tension within which romance emerges, and, like all our experiences, love and desire are partly constructions. They are not completely constructions, and they are certainly not subject to our conscious will. We do not wake up in the morning and decide whom we will love and desire that day. But love and desire arise within the textures of our daily lives, and we have a lot to do with constructing the contexts in which they appear.

Many cultures (including Western culture at an earlier point in history) establish a clear separation between marriage and the erotic. Marital "rights" are officially and legally established, and Eros is sought elsewhere, on terrain that makes it safer. These opposite categories are more easily recognizable as constructions, because they are social and institutional.

The widespread splitting between love and desire that Freud discerned at the beginning of the twentieth century and that is still very much with us at the beginning of the twenty-first is just as much a product of human constructions, but now on an individual, personal basis, largely outside of awareness. Whereas marital "rights" were at one time legal and official, marital "rights" and expectations are often now established unofficially but just as insistently, both consciously in the power negotiations of relationships and unconsciously in the identifications of self and partner with pseudomature stability and certainty. There is an easily available, abundant source of vicarious erotic excitement for sale. It is striking how much romance is sold in a degraded form in popular culture: soap operas, romance novels, fascination with the lives of celebrities. Having established deadness as a requirement for security in actual relationships, we seek passion vicariously in distant, safer realms.

In his theory of tragedy, Nietzsche captured the delicate balance, in the genuinely tragic, between the creation of forms and the dissolving of forms. Our individual lives, Nietzsche suggests, are transitory and in some sense illusory, ephemeral shapes that emerge from the energy that is the universe and that, in short order, are reabsorbed into the oneness. The enriching tragic in life can be missed in two ways. We can attribute to ourselves and our productions an illusory permanence, like a deluded builder of sandcastles who believes his creation is eternal. Or, alternatively, we can be defeated by our transience, unable to build, paralyzed as we wait for the tide to come in. Nietzsche envisions the tragic man or woman, living life to the fullest, as one who builds sandcastles passionately, all the time aware of the coming tide. The ephemeral, illusory nature of all form does not detract from the surrender to the passion of the work; it enhances and enriches it.

The genuinely romantic reflects this subtle blend of qualities that Nietzsche discovered in the tragic. The lover builds the castles of romance as if they would last forever, knowing full well they are fragile, transitory structures. And the splitting Freud termed "psychical impotence" is an effort to reduce the risk by segregating permanence from adventure. Those boring, sturdy castles over there will last forever; these other fanciful castles are only one-night stands. But in that splitting, something very important is lost. For authentic romance *is* tragic in Nietzsche's sense. It ends in death; it is never simply stable; at its best it comes and goes, perpetually lost and rediscovered. "Love dies or else lovers die," notes Harold Bloom in his discussion of *Romeo and Juliet,* "those are the pragmatic possibilities." Romantic passion requires a surrender to a depth of feeling that *should* come with guarantees. Unfortunately, there are no guarantees. Life and love are inevitably difficult and risky, and to control the risk we all struggle to locate and protect sources for both safety and adventure, often in different relationships.

There are surely relationships in which romantic passion dies over time; the price of abandoning them is often less than the price of endless years spent in resuscitation efforts. But the pull toward illusory certainties is very powerful. Passionlessness in long-term relationships is often a consequence not of the extinguishing of a flame but of collusive efforts to keep the relationship inert in a sodden stasis. I am not recommending the long-term relationship as a preferred state; it is a very hazardous condition. But of course that is also what sometimes makes such relationships interesting.

Human beings crave both security and adventure, both the familiar and the novel. We sometimes find ways to pursue these longings alternately, sometimes in a delicate balance with each other. Because they pull us in opposite directions, a balance between security and adventure can only be a transitory equilibrium, a temporary pause in our struggle to reconcile our conflictual longings.

Romance is filled with longing; intense desire always generates a sense of deprivation. The precondition of romantic passion is lack, desire for what one does not have. Yet romantic love entices us with the security it seems to promise: if only the lovers could find each other, be together, live happily ever after, then they would be safe and happy. So it is in the very nature of romantic passion to strive to overcome the lack it generates, to seek a wholeness that is rent by desire, to return to the castle with the damsel rescued from the dragon and make her the princess. We want to believe our castles are made of stone, not sand, our loves certain and secure, not subject to change over time. But back in our imagined castle, both the knight and the damsel, alas, often lose their allure.

The most obvious conclusion is that this particular man is not a real knight, this particular woman not a real princess after all. The real knight or princess is still out there somewhere, beyond the castle walls. But the most obvious conclusion is often obvious because it makes us feel temporarily safe rather than because it reflects the truth of our lives. It is not that knights, princesses, and castles are completely unreal, purely fantasies, but that knights, princesses, and castles are never the whole story when it comes to the shifting complexities and ambiguities of men and women and the social institutions we construct for ourselves.

Because we are always changing, love never stays the same. And thus romantic love is, by its very nature, destabilizing. It makes us dissatisfied with what we do have by pointing us always to something we don't quite have, or have enough of, or have dependably enough. In the next three chapters we will explore the ways in which each of the major dimensions of romantic passion—sexuality, idealization, and aggression—undermines our security and sense of self, and the ways in which that very destabilization raises the stakes and makes romantic love dangerous and meaningful.

2

The Strange Loops of Sexuality

Reciprocal love, such as I envisage it, is a system of mirrors which reflects for me, under the thousand angles that the unknown can take for me, the faithful image of the one I love, always more surprising in her divining of my own desire and more gilded with life.

—André Breton

NO REALM OF HUMAN EXPERIENCE is more fraught with conflict, conundrum, and confusion than sexuality. Sexual themes are prevalent in our music, theater, film, television, and literature. Sexual enticements and the promise of sexual happiness sell the products, from cars to computers, from clothes to toothpaste, that drive our economy. Clashing passionate convictions about sex are at the center of the "culture wars" that have dominated our public lives in recent decades, influencing elections and shaping the personae of our political and moral leaders. And conflicts around sexuality and its place in intimate relationships are a key feature of the struggle to make sense of our personal lives, an important part of what drives millions of people to self-help books, both New Age and traditional religions, therapies, and, most recently, chat rooms. What is it about sexuality that makes it so powerful and problematic to inhabitants of our culture?

What Is Sex?

We tend to be so preoccupied with sex in one way or another that we rarely take the time to consider what sex is and where it came from. Sexual reproduction appeared in the evolution of life on Earth because the intermingling of genetic material from two different organisms produced more adaptive results than the self-replication of a single organism. Lucky for us! So variations evolved that made sexual reproduction more interesting, that gave it motivational priority over other ways to spend one's time. Central to those variations were the evolution of genitals, body parts dense with nerve endings, producing intense pleasure when stimulated.

Despite their prominence in song lyrics, no one really knows what sex is actually like for birds and bees (except, perhaps, birds and bees). But by the time humans evolved sex was a lot more complicated than a mere commingling of bodies. Out of our bodies had emerged our quite extraordinary minds, and sexual events had become much more than somatic reflexes, taking on conceptual, emotional, psychological, and, some would say, spiritual dimensions. The very physical intensity of human sexual physiology requires a juxtaposition of persons, their excitements, their pleasures, their fantasies, their fears, their longings, their hopes—the entire range of mental life can come into play. The interpenetration of bodies required by the sexual act makes its endless variations ideally suited to represent desires, dreads, conflicts, and negotiations in the relations between self and others. Sexual experiences become powerful organizers of boundaries and self-representations. Bodily sensations and sensual pleasures delineate one's skin, one's outline, and the dialectics of bodily and sexual intimacies expose us, position us in relation to the other: over, under, inside, surrounding, against, yielding, controlling, adoring, enraptured, and so on. Because it provides such powerful material for emotional experience, sexual desire in humans has become our most intimate arena for personal and interpersonal expression.

For humans, bodies and minds are inseparable dimensions of sexual experiences. The colloquialism "fucking one's brains out" expresses a longing to simplify sexual experience by detaching soma from psyche, but that will never happen. And it is precisely the infusion of somatic events with psychological significance that makes our sexuality so dense with meanings and complications.

The Rudeness of Sex

Harold sought treatment partly because his wife was unable to cope any longer with the sexlessness of their marriage. There had been a brief period of sexual involvement early in their relationship but virtually none in the past several years, and Harold's wife, like most of us in our time, felt she was entitled to a satisfying sexual life. Harold's marriage was in deep trouble.

Harold was a beleaguered, dutiful husband, who lovingly admired his wife, wanted to make her happy, and felt ashamed of and diminished by his inability to fulfill what he regarded as his marital obligations. Yet, despite his initial attraction, he felt no desire for her now, and when he pushed himself through great effort to attempt sex, he was impotent. His sexuality was segregated into masturbation accompanied by pornography and fantasies involving slutty, instantly available women.

Harold was the only child of a racially mixed couple who lived a somewhat reclusive existence on the periphery of London. They had each suffered traumatic losses during childhood, and regarded themselves as not quite like other people. They had a tendency to feel overlooked, slighted, and they emphasized propriety, appearances, and manners. Harold's father became progressively alcoholic, and his mother became increasingly depressed. In the face of her husband's withdrawal, Harold's mother sometimes dressed in a sexually provocative manner, seemingly for Harold's benefit. She focused a great deal of attention upon him, and Harold became exquisitely sensitive to her moods; he could sense her depression even when they were in different rooms of their small apartment. As an adolescent Harold spent more and more time with friends, away from home, but he was never able to feel truly a part of things. He worked very hard to fit in, but always felt like an alien who was barely passing. The only instances of joy he later remembered from childhood were on solitary walks or rides on his bike, under a starry sky, the only moments in which he felt really free.

Harold wanted to have *had* sex with his wife more than he wanted to *have* sex with his wife. He found the route to sex with her exceedingly difficult, a "huge mountain," the traversing of which would require intense effort. The enormousness of the mountain as an obstacle was a powerful disincentive to even trying. Sex had long since ceased having anything to do with spontaneity; it was heavily burdened with effortfulness.

Many years of clinical work have confirmed for me the popular wisdom that sexuality requires chemistry: it can't be willed, and trying to will it is often a tragic waste of time. But for Harold, as for many people in long-term relationships, the chemistry *had* been there but seemed to have dissipated. The chemistry had been replaced by the mountain! But was it still behind the mountain? Under the mountain? Was there still a pulse?

An important part of the job of psychoanalysts is to interest their patients in the possibility that features of their world that they experience as powerful impediments to their pleasure and satisfaction, obstacles that seem completely outside their control and working against them, are actually their own constructions. The character of Penelope in Homer's *Odyssey* is a compelling portrayal of the way in which neurotic projects structure our lives. Penelope cannot remarry until she completes her weaving project; she weaves by day, so that her suitors feel she is making progress in choosing a husband, yet she unravels by night, hoping that her missing husband, Odysseus, will finally return. We all spend time both weaving and unraveling, but unlike Penelope we tend to be aware of only one side or the other of these carefully balanced projects. Harold was aware only of his efforts to scale the mountain; he was unaware of his ceaseless, unconscious mountain-building.

I noted that as soon as he established the mountain between himself and his wife, the possibility of sexual desire was gone. Here was this woman he had once found attractive, but now all he could sense was the mountain. I wondered what would happen if he stopped trying so hard, if he did less, not more. "There actually is no mountain," I suggested, except the one he unconsciously worked so hard to imagine. I asked him to consider whether or not he actually wanted the mountain, on whose slopes he so arduously toiled, to exist.

Harold came back next time reporting some sexual play with his wife. (He was now conscientiously working on the slopes of analysis instead of those of marriage.) As we explored his experiences, it became apparent that his focus in bed with his wife was exclusively on *her* sensations, *her* desires, *her* pleasures. What would it be like to forget about her needs, I asked, to give himself up to his own sensations, his own pleasure. He found this a preposterous question: he could never do it. I asked him to fantasize about what such a focus on his pleasure in her presence would be like. Thinking about it made him anxious; he would seem extremely selfish, he thought, indecent, unloving, unworthy, dangerous—the ultimate in rudeness. Pleasure, like the pleasure he took in his own existence as a boy on walks or bike rides or the pleasure he allowed himself in masturbation, was a solitary activity.

The feature of masturbation that made it so wonderful for him, we discovered, was that masturbation, perhaps more than any other activity, had no redeeming social value. No one else could possibly want him to do it, and that made it something, finally, that he could do for himself. Decency in the presence of another person required a hyperawareness of the other; to allow himself pleasure required an ability to be alone in the presence of another, which seemed to Harold the height of folly. The only sort of other in the presence of whom he could allow himself to surrender to his own pleasure was a fantasy other whom he omnipotently controlled, with no needs of her own. Only with such a fantasied other could Harold avoid the indecency, the inevitable offense to the other which his sexuality posed. Where Harold loved, he did not desire; where he desired, he could not love.

Why does sexuality come to feel indecent? We are going to consider two different approaches to this question: a traditional approach codified by Freud, and a new alternative. The first understands the human mind as composed of strata, the second of loops.

Freud's Human Animal

For Freud, sexuality is by its very nature antisocial, and, since we inevitably become thoroughly socialized, we are, fundamentally and profoundly, both antisocial and also social creatures.

But this vision of human nature did not begin with Freud. As far back as Plato, human beings portrayed themselves to themselves as hybrid creatures, like the unicorn, the sphinx, the griffin. We are composites, with a lower nature driven by bodily appetites, passions, and instincts and a higher nature in which reason, devotion, and spirituality hold sway.

For Freud, drawing on Darwin, we ascended from below, rising from evolutionarily "lower" forms of life to attain consciousness, reason, and civilized morality. Our evolution, however, is incomplete. We remain composites, in our very bodies and minds, halfway between animals and angels. Stratification of higher and lower was a central motif, a kind of conceptual signature, in the way Freud understood virtually all significant areas of emotional life. His well-known structural model is a miniaturized, interiorized battleground upon which biology clashes with culture in unconscious conflicts: the id is the deep repository of our natural instincts; the superego is the internalized representative of culture; the ego mediates between them.

Freud regarded sexuality (later adding aggression) as the motivational lower stratum, the primitive impulses that fuel all the higher levels of the mind. Across his many different models of mind and conceptual reworkings of human psychodynamics, Freud always saw an inescapable tension between our human nature, revealed in our sexuality and aggression, and our transformation into the higher, civilized creatures we have tried to become. As he put it in 1916, "Society must undertake as one of its most important educative tasks to tame and restrict the sexual instinct . . . for with the complete irruption of the sexual instinct, educability is for practical purposes at an end. Otherwise the instinct would break down every dam and wash away the laboriously erected work of civilization."

Despite all the Freud-bashing of recent years, despite all the objections and questions that have been raised about classical psychoanalytic theory, Freud's vision of the human animal has been remarkably influential and, to one degree or another, has seeped into the ways all of us experience and think about our bodies and our sexuality. Of course we struggle with sexuality: our sexual nature drives us toward excess, indecency, and indiscriminate gratification; our ideals and social norms require us to be decent, controlled, and regulated. Our sexuality is the animal within us. Depending on your point of view, and there are several passionately held points of view, our sexual nature needs to be either tamed, quarantined, or liberated.

The assumption of the demonic primitiveness of sexuality is the key feature of one of the most common understandings of the tendency of romance to become degraded. Romantic passion is, like human beings, necessarily a composite phenomenon, an uneasy union of lofty ideals and base instincts. In this traditional understanding, Harold's love for his wife and his sexuality are, by their very nature, incommensurate. To bridge them, either his love needs to become less devoted or his sexuality needs to be tamed.

However, this vision of the human organism as stratified, composed of primitive instincts and biology below and rationality and spirituality above, this time-worn vision of our hybrid nature has, in recent decades, started to fray. We are very used to thinking about ourselves in this traditional, stratified way. To prepare the ground for an alternative approach, we need to consider recent shifts in thinking about, first, the relationship between the biological and the social and, second, the nature of nature itself.

The Human Animal Today

In Freud's time, the animal and the cultured in us were conceived of as deriving from different sources (internal and external, respectively) and layered in our experience. In recent decades, the biological and the social (and the linguistic) are understood to thoroughly interfuse each other. It is our biological, animal nature to speak, to form societies, and to generate cultures. What may be the most distinctive feature of human evolution from earlier primate species is the formation of specifically human social relations, cultural and linguistic groups. What Freud regarded as secondary, external influences many now regard as essential to our nature. From this perspective, no less Darwinian than Freud's, we are not animal first and then social; we are profoundly, deeply *social animals*.

Human beings form relationships; we create and preserve linguistic communities. Why? Are communities and the linguistic communication that knits them together the products of discrete needs, perhaps basic drives? No. It is much more than that. Defining humans as relational is quite different from specifying gregariousness or sociability as a specific drive among other drives, like the need for food or the need to reproduce. Consider an analogy.

Human beings are oxygen-breathing organisms; we are not *driven* to seek oxygen (except if it is suddenly withdrawn). It is simply what we are built to do, and we do it without trying to do it or doing it as a means to other ends. Human beings are also language-generating creatures. In the heyday of behaviorism, language was assumed to be an instrumental act that emerged in the individual for some purpose, because it was reinforced. Now language is generally regarded as an *emergent* property of the human brain. Thus Steven Pinker describes language as an instinct precisely because people know how to talk in more or less the sense that spiders know how to spin webs . . . spiders spin spider webs because they have spider brains, which give them the urge to spin and the competence to succeed.

There are many controversial theories about the evolutionary adaptive purpose or purposes which originally, eons ago, selected for language development. But, Pinker is suggesting, the young spider begins to spin his web not because he is hungry or because he intuits his need for webs as the basis of his livelihood, but because spinning webs is what he is designed to do. Similarly, human babies generate sounds, and eventually language, not for some instrumental purpose, but because they have human brains, and that is what we humans have been designed, over the course of our evolution, to do.

Human beings, starting as small babies, seek other human minds to interact with, not for the satisfaction of some discrete need, but because we are wired to respond visually to the human face, olfactorily to human smells, auditorily to the human voice, and semiotically to human signs. We are designed, in many, many ways we are just beginning to appreciate, to be drawn into interaction with other human beings, and these interactions are necessary for babies to be able to use their brains to become specifically human, language-generating creatures, with specifically human minds.

Thus we do not begin as sexual creatures who encounter social constraints. We begin as bodily/social creatures, and our sexuality is as profoundly, deeply cultural as it is physical. Human sexuality emerges within relational and linguistic contexts. Behaviorally, sexual acts can take place with or without other people. But psychologically, the meanings of sexuality derive from social structures, interpersonal forms of relatedness, and linguistic categories.

For example, for some people mutual sexual arousal is the most intimate activity imaginable. And yet, for Harold, sexual pleasure entailed a self-absorption that obliterated his awareness of the other: mutual sexual arousal was unimaginable. And there are many other possibilities. The same behavioral or physiological event (a touch, arousal, orgasm) has distinct, often very different textures of meaning in different minds. For some people orgasm is a transcendent, blissful experience; for others it is a shattering, terrifying disintegration. Freud and his contemporaries could assume they knew what sex *was* for any particular person, because it came prepackaged in animal instincts. We can never assume we know what sex *is* for any one of us, because it becomes *human* sexuality only in a particular social and linguistic context that creates its meanings.

The traditional vision of mind as layered derived from the premise that our sexuality is a demonic expression of our prehuman ancestry that is a phylogenetic legacy, still intact, that exerts an autonomous force within us. But we are increasingly realizing that our bodies and our cultural creations thoroughly interpenetrate each other—they bring each other to life and also constrain each other. There is no sexuality or aggression or any other bodily experience that is unmediated by social and linguistic shaping. And conversely, we experience all social and linguistic influence as embodied creatures, with bodies that have particularly human parts and a particularly human configuration.

One of the most powerful images of this contemporary understanding of the unity of mind and body is M. C. Escher's drawing of two hands. Each hand draws an image out of which emerges a hand which in turn draws the other hand: body generates imagination generates body generates imagination.

The Nature of Nature

Until fairly recently it seemed pretty clear what nature is: nature is the world, untouched by people, the world outside the perimeter of human culture, the world as it was before we started altering it.

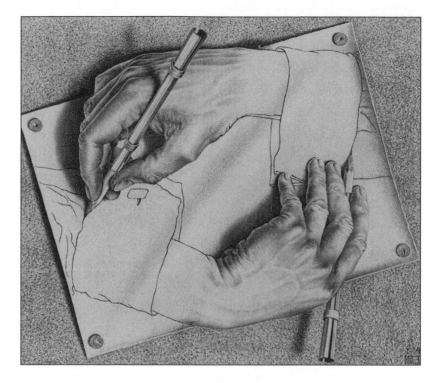

M. C. Escher, "Drawing Hands"

And our sexuality is a piece of that nature residing within us.

However, we've come to realize how socially constructed are our very ideas about "nature." Nature is a harmonious garden. Nature is "red in tooth and claw." Natural man is a barbarian. Natural man is a noble savage. How can we decide which description of nature is right? A great deal depends on who is conjuring up nature, at what time in history, in what cultural context, for what purpose. The appearance of menageries and zoos was concurrent with urbanization, and our ideas of the "wilderness" have always served as a counterpoint, an inverted image, of the current state of civilization. Linguistic analysis suggests that the word "nature," despite its connotations of simplicity, is "perhaps the most complex word in the [English] language."

But surely we can find nature, our nature at least prior to nurture, in the wiring with which human beings begin life, before experience and culture alters it. However, the traditional dichotomy of nature versus nurture that has dominated Western philosophy and psychology has been profoundly challenged by recent advances in neurophysiology. The stratification model of human experience—biology versus culture, nature versus nurture—was predicated on the assumption that human biology was a complete package at birth, when the biologically wired newborn presented herself ready for the secondarily formative impact of culture. Constitution was established during gestation; cultural experience was now poised to lay down a second layer.

It turns out that much of the wiring that will *become* the biology, the very constitution, of the adult is *not* present at birth, but is laid down in the first few years of life, in the social, linguistic, familial, interpersonal, nurturing context that the infant requires for survival. The brain of the newborn, we now know, is only partially developed. Nerve cells and neural pathways are incomplete at birth; they are shaped to a considerable extent by the baby's experience with others. Patterns of arousal and quiescence, thresholds of excitation and relaxation, diurnal rhythms—many features of what used to be understood as purely inborn temperament or constitution—are now understood to be partly shaped in early interactions with caregivers. We have come to appreciate how formative those early years are, how much culture is wired into our very bodies. Biology and culture, nature and nurture do not constitute separable layers or levels but suffuse each other in the establishment of neural pathways in early development.

Freud imagined sexuality in its raw state as rapacious and indiscriminate, and his libido theory was the most comprehensive development of the notion, spanning many centuries, that human sexuality, a version of animal sexuality, is a relentless, spontaneously arising propulsive force. As we now know, animal sexuality is remarkably varied and is not driven continuously from within. Much of animal sexuality is distinctly phasic (estrus cycles) and contextual (responsive to specific stimuli). No animal of which I am aware, certainly not our nearest primate relatives, even comes close to being as sexually obsessed as human beings.

The traditional derivation of the inherent delicacy and instability of romance from the primitiveness of sexuality has been, for decades, aesthetically and morally satisfying. It has helped us partially disown what we often don't like about ourselves by locating it in an unwanted legacy, forced upon us by our animal ancestors. We have personified nature to enable us to locate within it those aspects of our own experience that we have difficulty bearing. We've taken troubling aspects of distinctly human sexuality and created anthropomorphic images of animal sexuality and nature; we have then concluded that this primitive force, the one we have imagined as a dark shadow of our own phylogenetic ancestry, is the source of our problems.

But it is no longer possible to regard Harold's rude sexuality as something *in* him or *beneath* his social self; it *is* Harold, or at least one version of him; it is as much a social construction as is his bicycle riding. It was shaped in the subtle interactions between Harold and his parents, particularly in the interplay between his bodily responses and his mother's confusing provocativeness, intrusiveness, and preoccupation with manners. We need another way to understand the splitting of Harold's psyche and the segregation of his excitement.

From Layers to Strange Loops

One of my favorite metaphors for thinking about the paradoxes of human experience is Douglas R. Hofstadter's image, in his remarkable book *Godel, Escher, Bach: An Eternal Golden Braid*, of the

M. C. Escher, "Relativity"

"strange loop," which he demonstrates is fundamental to the "incompleteness theorem" of Godel's mathematics, the dizzying visual images of Escher, and the fugal structure developed by Bach. The "Strange Loop phenomenon occurs," Hofstadter explains, "whenever, by moving upwards (or downwards) through the levels of some hierarchical system, we unexpectedly find ourselves right back where we started." On Escher's stairs, for example, the climbers seem to ascend, step by step, only to discover themselves once again where they began, having completed the journey yet starting over at the same time.

The defining characteristic of the human mind, Hofstadter argues, is a particular kind of strange loop in which there is "an interaction between levels in which the top level reaches back down towards the bottom level and influences it, while at the same time being itself determined by the bottom level." In the human mind, the material substrate of the brain, our "hardware" (some people call it "wetware") generates mental processes, our "software," that loop back to change the "hardware" in our brains, which generates different programs or processes that in turn change our brains in continuing cycles. We can experience emotions like anger, anxiety, and sexual excitement only because we have the neural equipment that generates such emotions. Yet these emotions themselves generate brain states, the chemistry of which affects neural pathways and function. We can compose life plans because we have the neural equipment that makes possible such cognitive projects. Yet the plans themselves (exercising, taking medicinal and recreational drugs, meditating) affect neural pathways and neural function, influencing the kinds of plans we may compose in the future. We are, in the language of Hofstadter's world of artificial intelligence, self-programming computers.

Hofstadter's strange loops are helpful as we visualize the shift from the traditional view of biology and culture, nature and nurture, as separable, stratified components of human experience to the more contemporary view in which biology and culture, body and mind, interfuse each other. Our bodies generate mental states in which we experience feelings that themselves affect our brain chemistry. Our evolution as physical creatures has made possible the development of human culture and language, which in turn generate the ideas and metaphors through which we experience our bodies. These ways of experiencing our bodies actually change our bodies. The language and cultural sophistication that have emerged from our material existence have produced the metaphors of sexuality as bestial and as a propulsive force as a way of accounting for intense, conflictual, uneasy aspects of human sexuality. Looping back, that metaphor in turn has been an important shaper of the ways in which people across the centuries (Harold, for example) have experienced and treated their bodies and their sexuality.

One casualty of these developments in our understanding of the interpenetration of biology and culture is what now seems the anachronistic, almost quaint notion that there is some sort of precultural human sexuality. It is difficult to imagine how we might isolate sexuality in a pure, natural state before our language, social structures, and personal imaginations have transformed it into the forms through which we experience it. This does not diminish the importance of biology and the ways it has been shaped over the course of evolution, but our biology operates in inextricable conjunction with cultural phenomena.

Picture the convergence of two streams in the creation of a whirlpool. Before they meet, it is possible to isolate and describe the waters of each separately. After they meet, their drops are interfused. It is no longer possible to dip a cup into the whirlpool and separate what has come from each stream. Nature and nurture operate in a similar fashion. They do not appear in human experience in pure form, isolated from each other. They are two currents that become completely mixed. This makes implausible the traditional notion that attributes the fragility of romance, its tendency toward degradation, to the rapaciousness of unconstrained sexuality. We don't find particles of pure, unconstructed sexuality. There aren't any. Perhaps another crazy loop might offer more illumination of what makes sexuality so potentially destabilizing: the loop comprising our dual existence as both personal and interpersonal creatures.

Self/Other

We emerge out of and are saturated with relations with others, yet we (in Western culture) organize our experience into selves with what feel like distinct, inviolable interiors, with boundaries, partly negotiable and partly nonnegotiable. Much of the complexity of sexuality and its relation to romance derives from the deep significance of the tension between the personal and the relational, between "oneness" and "twoness."

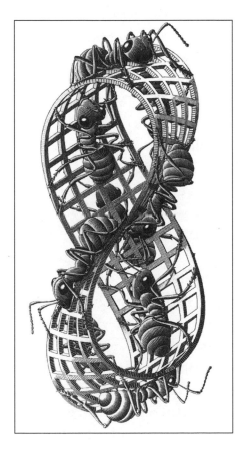

M. C. Escher, "Mobius Strip I"

The strange loops of biology and culture are generally portrayed as vertical: lower generates higher, which circles around to alter lower. But I would like to turn this image on its side, to imagine a *horizontal* strange loop as a conceptual device for thinking about the relationship between oneness and twoness, the personal and the relational, self and other. In the beginning, we might say, is the relational, social, linguistic matrix in which we discover ourselves, or, as Heidegger vividly put it, into which we are "thrown." Within that matrix are formed, precipitated out, individual psyches with subjectively experienced interior spaces. Those subjective spaces begin as microcosms of the relational field; interpersonal relationships are internalized and transformed into a distinctly personal experience. Those personal experiences are, in turn, regulated and transformed, generating new interpersonal forms that alter macrocosmic patterns of interaction. Interpersonal relational processes generate private, interior processes, which reshape interpersonal processes, which reshape intrapsychic processes, on and on in a self-propelling strange loop, an endless Mobius Strip in which internal and external are perpetually regenerating and transforming themselves and each other.

Sex (along with death) is surely among the most private of experiences. Yet for many people the most intense forms of sexual experience are available only in the interpenetration of bodies made possible by sexual engagements with others: in fantasies, in feelings, and in actions. And there is probably no domain of human experience in which both the interpenetrability of and the tension between the personal and the social are more acutely experienced than in sexuality.

The traditional model of mind as stratified helped explain both the adventure and the risk of sexuality. Sex exposes our lower, bestial layers and challenges our standards of social decency. But, as we shall see, the real adventure and risk of sexuality stem from the breach it creates in the conventional boundaries between self and other. We establish decency in intimate relationships to facilitate continuity, security, and attachment. But bodily states and pleasures are full of surprises. What is at risk of being considered indecent in the exposures of sex is not the beast in us but the *me-ness* in us.

Is *Sex Quite So Private?*

Ironically, the density of genital nerve endings, selectively designed over the course of mammalian and primate evolution to power the urge to reproduce, also lends an interiority and elusiveness to sexual experience. The corporeal intensity of sexual arousal and gratification, its very power, contributes to its utter privacy. Although it is one of our most common experiences, none of us knows quite what sex is like for anyone else. The very regularity of the bodily equipment belies the highly distinctive forms through which sexuality becomes personalized over the course of a life. The more or less standard equipment has been hijacked by the human imagination.

One of the more enduring features of Freud's explorations of human sexuality was his discovery that, unlike Gertrude Stein's roses, sex is not sex is not sex. *Psycho*sexuality, as Freud discovered, is not definable by the sexual event itself. In psychical impotence, the act may be performable, but without a fullness of desire and gratification. Psychoanalysis revealed the radical interiority of sexuality as well as its opaqueness to others and, to some extent, to the subject himself.

The startling durability of pornography as a human diversion surely results in part from a voyeuristic longing to find out what sex is like for others; the recurring disappointment of pornography results from the perpetual rediscovery that one never will. The sexual experience, despite, or perhaps because of, its intensity, can only be known from the inside. Thus Louise, the frustrated and bullied housewife of the film *Thelma and Louise* notes, after her first genuinely erotic lovemaking with a larcenous stranger, "Now I know what all the fuss was about."

It has become politically dangerous to derive psychological differences between men and women from anatomical differences, but the existential psychoanalytic essayist Leslie Farber wrote during less wrought times. He argued that because sexual intercourse requires a highly visible erection from a man, because orgasm renders that erection inoperative for a time, and because the signs of female arousal and orgasm are so much subtler and more easily simulated, sexual insecurity and jealousy are much more profound for men than for women. The first-person experience of sex is unknowable for another, but, Farber suggests, it is more unknowable in the woman than in the man. A woman can feel she has "had" a man after intercourse, whereas a man never really knows for sure. The possibility of effective faking raises the stakes and made Meg Ryan's convincing simulated orgasm in the restaurant scene of the film *When Harry Met Sally* a classic of modern cinematic history, simultaneously comical and horrifying. "I'll have what she's having," says her fellow customer to the waiter. Don't we all wish we could omnipotently order subjective experiences, both for ourselves and for our partners. This male-female difference is what drives the perpetual question for many men, long after an appreciation of its anti-erotic impact has squelched its actual utterance: "Did you come?" We each long to know of the other: Where *are* you in there? How does this experience with me compare with your experiences with other lovers? What are the subtle textures of the sensations, the fantasies, the unconscious resonances? And each of us knows that our own sexual experience is at least partly ineffable, indemonstrable, private.

Because it is never simply a biological, reflexive action but always partially an act of imagination, sexuality, one's own or that of another, can never be fixed and wholly predictable. In this sense, there is always an unknown, an otherness in the experience of sexuality in both one's partner and in oneself. This unknown and unknowable dimension of sexual passion contributes to both its excitement and its risks. It is part of what makes sexuality potentially destabilizing. The kind of "knowing" that often kills passion in long-term love relationships, the certainty that the accessibility and depth of engagement of one's partner and oneself is a sure thing, entails the superimposition of an illusory transparency and stasis upon something that is, by its very nature, elusive and shifting.

Part of what makes us think of sexuality as deeply personal and private is the sense that it surges up from within us. One of the defining features of the common understanding of sexuality (formalized in Freud's libido theory in the early years of the twentieth century) was that sexuality is an endogenous push from inside, originating in somatic tissues. Our bodies *need* to take in nutriment; the urge increases over time until satisfied. Our bodies *need* to vacate waste products; the urge increases over time until satisfied. Many people think that sex works in the same fashion. Evolution has designed us with sexual and aggressive instincts for survival purposes, and the urges deriving from those needs push us from inside. Time intensifies those needs, it is believed, and the urges increase until satisfied. Thus Freud thought we *seek* objects for gratification because of the buildup of the sexual (as well as the aggressive) drive. Of course not any object will do. Specific libidinal and aggressive objects become linked with gratification of drives through early associative experiences. Within this line of thinking, sex begins, like hunger, with the push from within, generating a tension that secondarily seeks specific objects for release.

But this is certainly not the whole story. Others have great power not only to gratify sexual desire but to arouse it as well. Others can reach and excite us through virtually every sense: through touch and sight, the more traditional modalities, but also through sound (as the phenomenon of phone sex has made apparent) and smell (as the recent research on pheromones has revealed). With mounting arousal, sex certainly *becomes* a powerful push from within, but we are wired to be exquisitely responsive to stimulation by others. Surely Freud was right to think that much sexual desire arises spontaneously, in the absence of an arousing object, but we need to look more closely to discover whether what appears to be a spontaneous eruption of desire in the body is really *body*-generated or *self*-generated. Psychoanalytic explorations of human subjectivity in recent years have alerted us to the ways in which we perpetually regenerate our experience through both conscious and unconscious fantasy.

We do not awaken each morning to encounter a brand-new world; we anticipate that today's world will be populated by the same cast of characters as yesterday's. We expect to find the same enticements, the same dangers, the same rewards, the same disappointments. The external world we maneuver around in is always partially an imaginative re-creation of our inner world, and those others whom we perpetually regenerate continue, each day, to anchor, soothe, challenge, threaten, outrage, arouse, satisfy, and torment us. Self is so deeply implicated with others that the most private, interior experiences are linked with and shaped by, on both conscious and unconscious levels, implicit others.

When Susan (whom we met in Chapter 1) experiences sexual yearning for her lover, the longing does not simply bubble up from bodily tissues but emerges in the context of a subjective world she has constructed and maintained, the centerpiece of which is her secure and numbing attachment to her cozy husband. When Harold finds himself in a pornographic reverie, the excitement emerges in the context of a subjective world organized around the mountain of obligations that mediate his attachment to his wife. Thus as we enter more deeply into the privacy of the self, the recesses of interiority, we find ourselves encountering, on our horizontal strange loop, a plethora of otherness.

Are Others Really So "Other"?

What of the second side of the dialectic between self and other that fires eroticism, the enticements of what philosophers call "alterity"? Poets, philosophers, and psychoanalytic theorists have suggested that the central feature of sexual passion is the transcendence of the self, of the familiar boundaries of one's own experience—the sense of reaching and being reached by, penetrating and being penetrated by another. But clearly not just any form of not-self will do; each of us has a "type" or types, a distinctive form of otherness that provides just the right chemistry.

Otherness and sameness are opposites, and we think of opposites as if they are irrelevant to each other, as if they have nothing to do with each other. But opposites have a great deal to do with each other. They often imply each other; in some sense they are built into each other. Light presupposes dark, and vice versa. The very concept of up presupposes a sense of down, and vice versa. Many of our basic concepts are implicitly defined by their opposites so precisely that they are meaningful, in yin/yang fashion, only as contrasts, as complementarities. Much of the otherness we seek from and find exciting in romantic partners operates in this fashion. Opposites attract, we are told. Opposites attract because they are inversions of each other, the same thing in different forms. Otherness, in this way of thinking, might be redefined, not as what is truly alien to the self, but as what has been squelched, truncated, disallowed in the self. (Jung called these disclaimed features of the self "the shadow.") And because self is defined so centrally in terms of non-self, otherness, the kind of otherness that fires erotic passion, might be considered a *form* of self, a mirror image.

Often starkly drawn polarities, with conventional gender implications, are central to both heterosexual and homosexual passion: hard/soft, powerful/yielding, independent/dependent, top/bottom, tough/tender, and so on. But there are many other kinds of contrasts distributed in complex ways within couples that reflect this same sort of mirror-image complementarity: refined/vulgar, cultivated/innocent, flamboyant/simple, expressive/restrained, and so on. What is alluring in the other may not be the otherness of the other as much as the opportunity for making contact, at a safe distance, with disclaimed aspects of the self. Much of the futility so prevalent in romance derives from the way sameness often masquerades as otherness. We believe we are escaping our selves, redressing our pasts, but the partners we choose as accomplices in these would-be acts of freedom, announcing themselves as different and new, are often, in fact, not so different, not so new.

We all have a tendency to reproduce our miseries with extraordinary consistency. In love relations, we approach each new relationship as the antidote to the problems of the last one, and, with daunting regularity, each new relationship turns out to be a new version of the old one(s). This is sometimes attributed to the uncanniness of the unconscious in locating childhood oedipal objects. The man who dreads certain features of his mother manages to find a woman who, despite appearances to the contrary, is a replica of her. The woman who idealizes one parent and despises the other manages to find a man who appears to have the desirable parental attributes only to reveal, over time, precisely the despised qualities.

But all this is really not so mysterious or uncanny. The great irony of many relationships is that the presenting feature of the other person, the quality for which we chose that person, often operates in his or her own psychic economy as a defense against precisely its opposite. The partner selected for his seemingly impressive stability may be defending himself against a chaotic recklessness; the partner chosen for her liveliness may be defending against an underlying depression; the partner chosen for his high moral values may be defending against a secret fascination with the perverse; and the partner chosen for her sexiness may be covering up a deep sense of deadness and impairment, may herself be waiting to be brought to life. Thus the otherness of the other we choose as an antidote to previous relationships, as well as the other we choose for what appears to be complementarity to our self, often reveals, beneath the exaggerated surface, precisely the quality we were hoping to escape. When we give ourselves over to loving somebody, it is not just them we are discovering and loving but who we are and who we will become when we are with them.

For Harold, where was sex on the strange loop of self/other? The other person was so demanding a presence that a surrender to his own pleasure in her proximity was unthinkable. He felt that placing his penis inside her was an act of utter rudeness, indecency, and callous exploitation. But who was this "other" who cast her shadow so powerfully over his existence? Originally the other was his mother, or, more precisely, his little boy's experience of his mother, with all her attentiveness and all her problems. But this original other now resided as an internal presence inside him, and his experience of new others in his adult life, such as his wife, was greatly colored by his earlier attachment to his mother. In the loopiness of self and other,

Harold now constructed his experience of his wife according to his own internal requirements, insisting on a powerful, coercive (m)other whom he dutifully served, because she was an external replica of the presence in his own inner world of the security-providing residue of his experience of his mother. And in the isolation Harold sought for his solitary pleasures, he was not really alone; in the loopiness of self and other, he allowed himself to expose and surrender to his private sexual excitement in a world populated by perpetually available and controlled women and an embracing universe.

Surrender and Control

The sense of surrender is central to romance, and here too the loopiness of self and other—or by now we might want to call it self/other—plays an important part. Love is intoxicating, bewitching; it works its magic on us. We speak of "falling in love," getting "turned on," being struck like Michael Corleone in *The Godfather* by a "thunderbolt." Intense erotic excitement feels as if it originates in a force outside the self, beyond one's own agency, a force that destabilizes one's ordinary self and undermines one's customary sense of agentic control. "I am in love," says the Elvis Presley lyric, "I'm all shook up." It is the allure of surrender that makes passion inevitably dangerous. Passion is unpredictable, unbidden, outside the willful, omnipotent control we struggle to maintain over our lives.

The loopiness of the complex relations between self and others (or selves and other) sheds some light on why the subjective experience of sexuality as bestial is so common. To be bestial suggests an inhumane disregard of other persons, an exploitation of them for one's own purposes, a purely animalistic (in our anthropomorphization and secret romanticization of animals) use of them for our own pleasure. We are more comfortable thinking of the beast *within* us than of the beast that sometimes *is* us. To be bestial is to throw off the constraints of one's own personality and to depersonalize the other. To be bestial may promise a way of reaching the other more fundamentally or freeing oneself from the other's claims. Being bestial together can offer a mutual use of each other in a freedom from personality and social constraints, providing an intensity and immediacy that may not be possible in the subtle choreography of other forms of human intimacy.

French novelists and philosophers have compared the experience of sexual orgasm to death *(la petite morte)*. I have always had difficulty understanding this as anything more than an abstract literary conceit, because sensuality and orgasm seem to me so much an intensification of life rather than death. But the death implicated in eroticism might be thought of as a loss not of life but of structure, and this sheds light on another facet of the dialectics of self/other.

Becoming a person entails self-organization; no matter how rich and multiplicitous it is, no matter how "true" or authentic, self-structure forecloses and truncates many dimensions of experience. Density and complexity are inevitably sacrificed in favor of simplicity and dependability. In the very distinction between self and not-self, a grid is superimposed upon the complex interpenetrability between self and other. Loss of richness, immersion, and density is an inevitable feature of development, of becoming *a* person. This loss has been expressed in many different ways, perhaps most powerfully in Wordsworth's poetic vision, in "Intimations of Mortality," of the loss of a childhood "trailing clouds of glory": "nothing can bring back the hour / Of splendour in the grass, of glory in the flower." In all these formulations, both pathological *and* healthy self-development generate loss and, perhaps, a longing for return, expansion, relief from the strain of psychic structure itself.

This self-surrendering function of romantic love is dramatically illustrated by the most famous lover of them all, Shakespeare's Romeo. *Romeo and Juliet* opens with a discussion by his worried relatives about the lovesick Romeo. We soon learn, however, that the object of our hero's affections is not Juliet, whom he has yet to meet, but Rosaline, who is sworn to abstinence. Early in the play Romeo waxes lyrical over Rosaline's superlative charms: "The all-seeing sun / Ne'er saw her match since first the world begun." How quickly things change when Romeo meets Juliet later that day: "Did my heart love till now? Forswear it, sight! / For I ne'er saw true beauty till this night." Romeo, we begin to suspect, is more in love with being in love than with either woman. And the mutual self-annihilation of the play's tragic ending is a surrender not so much to a particular other as to selflessness itself.

The transcendent power of sexuality might be understood as emanating precisely from its potential to undermine everyday psychic structure, to destabilize the ordinary experience of self. There are multiple surrenders, relinquishments of self-control, involved in powerful sexual experiences, romantic or otherwise: the surrender of self to another, placing oneself in the other's hands, to arouse, frustrate, tease, gratify; the surrender of agentic control to one's own bodily sensations and processes, to the unexpected surprises of physicality; the surrender of one's ordinary self to other potential selves emerging in fantasy, in one's immersion in the sensations and rhythms of the other.

In romantic love the distinct otherness of the other becomes more important. What distinguishes eroticism from less complex, casual sexuality is precisely an other experienced as at least partly elusive, enticing, both there and not there. What makes intense desire, sexual and otherwise, so dangerous is that it entails a longing for something important from a unique someone whom one has allowed to become important. It is the specificity of the other that leads to risk, the allure of another subject outside one's control that creates such intense vulnerability; the lover then inevitably generates an array of magical devices, efforts to establish control over the other through a fantasied omnipotence.

At the extreme end of this continuum are sexual perversions, the central feature of which is the degradation of the other to an object under one's omnipotent control, so that the sexual act becomes a perseverative script in which nothing new can ever happen. But we are all involved in efforts to regulate the risks of desire in less absolute, subtler ways. We seek stability, predictability and dependability; we become attached, and we want the objects of our attachment to stay fixed, unchanging. So, ironically enough, attachment is the great enemy of eroticism. The senses of excess, enigma, mystery—displaced, from early childhood, by parents anxious to provide security—constitute the very sexiness of eroticism, and these are precisely the qualities we tend to work so hard to eliminate from ordinary life as adults, from primary relationships, from what we want to believe are "secure" attachments.

It is generally thought that sexual fantasies reveal what the fantasizers *really want to do,* had they the opportunity or courage. However, often fantasies express precisely what the fantasizers do *not* want to do. Certain activities can be exciting to think about *as* fantasies, in the freedom of imagination, although as actual behaviors they would be repugnant. Bringing our various conflictual wishes and fantasies into our relationship with the person on whom we depend can seem much more difficult and dangerous than limiting our fantasies to unknown others, pretending it is only with them, not with our partner, that we might wish to do what we fantasize.

Another Other

Some people have great difficulty in allowing themselves to become aroused unless the other with whom they are involved initiates sexuality or pursues it with obvious abandon. Like all intense emotions, sexual arousal is contagious, and mutual excitement is reciprocally stimulating. But there is often another factor at work. For some people, their own intense excitement is too conflictual, too dirty or reckless, too rude or aggressive, for them to feel comfortable displaying it in the presence of another, particularly another whom they love and respect. So they need the other to go first, or to respond with an immediate, reassuring sign that the sex is acceptable. In extreme cases, only another type of other will do. Thus women (and also gay men) who are attracted only to crude, defiant, dangerous men may require the other's outlaw status as a prerequisite to allowing themselves to feel their own desire. And men (and gay women) who are attracted only to slutty, sexually provocative women may require the other's open endorsement of explicit sexuality as a prerequisite to allowing themselves to experience their own excitement.

George sought treatment because of intense unhappiness in his marriage of ten years. Although he loved his wife and young child, he had come to regard his wife as unbearably controlling and to feel claustrophobically trapped. Her various demands, such as an insistence on his calling to let her know when he would be late for dinner, had come to feel intolerably coercive. He found sexual liaisons with other women irresistible and felt increasingly disaffected from his wife.

With some embarrassment George eventually revealed that among the most intense of his sexual adventures were regular visits to several madams who played the role of dominatrix with him. In these encounters he would place himself totally in the woman's hands. She could order him around, tie him up, do anything she wanted to him. He would beg and plead for mercy and release, to no avail. Although there was rarely any genital contact or orgasms, George found these encounters extraordinarily thrilling. I was struck by the odd irony of a man who found his wife's demand for common courtesy oppressive placing himself under the control of a virtual stranger. George explained that the women's control was a dramatic fiction. The way it worked in this sort of relationship was that they would establish a code word before beginning. He could beg and scream for mercy without effect, but if he said the code word the play would stop instantly. He was really in total control, and it was that complete power that made it possible for him to pretend that the woman was in control.

As we came to understand it, the control George resented from his wife was a control he longed for and yet was terrified he would surrender himself to. Because he actually depended on his wife for so much, even minor concessions like a phone call seemed too dangerous. He could only let himself surrender, in a perversely contrived scenario, to someone with whom he had nothing at stake. Much later I asked him how he was so sure that the dominatrix would, in fact, comply with the code word. Of course, there was economic power as a background factor. But there seemed to be a leap of faith involved as well, one that he carefully did not notice. Even financial dominance is complex, and desire is always risky; actual, as opposed to fantasized, control is difficult to come by. He believed he was in control, imagining himself under her control. But from another perspective, he *was* under her control, imagining himself to be in control in order to pretend that he was surrendering. Because human relationships are built around such complex interdependencies, control and predictability often take on this sort of nesting-doll quality.

For George, the surrender to the other's power to arouse and gratify was terrifying. With his wife, who was important to him in many ways, and on whom he was therefore dependent, he could feel safe by continually disappointing her expectations of him, imagining himself perpetually dancing beyond her control. With the dominatrix, he could surrender to his own excitement at her total control over him only by constructing, with her help, a fantasy of his total control over her.

Veronica was an attractive woman in her early forties who sought treatment because she regarded her history of promiscuity as a threat to her marriage. She had grown up in Atlanta, one of five children of a tough, openly philandering, abusive police captain and his long-suffering, depressed wife. Her father ran the family with an iron fist and was particularly controlling of his daughters, whom he warned against any adventures with men. Veronica and her sister became adept at arranging sexual escapades and collaborating on complex cover stories, about which the father would interrogate them separately, to see if their stories would match. It was as if sex were an extremely exciting, dangerous, destructive activity available only to the father.

As an adult Veronica was drawn to wealthy, fast-living men she regarded as powerful; attracting and sustaining their desire was enormously compelling. However, she herself could become aroused during sex only if she concocted a fantasy of *another* woman, not her, having sex with her lover. She would picture the other woman as being terribly exciting to the man, making him "lose it" in sexual abandon. In previous relationships, when she feared a diminution of her lover's sexual interest, she had arranged with escort services for another woman to act out this scenario.

Veronica loved her husband and dreaded both what she saw as the inevitable diminution of his passion for her and her compulsion to seek out and excite more powerful men. Her intense ambivalence toward her father in childhood seemed to have left her with an inability to locate and own her pleasure, which was forever hostage to the man, whose desire she would perseveratively arouse, gratify, and disclaim.

The omnipotence of repetitive fantasies often makes possible a particular juxtaposition of self-with-other which would risk annihilation of self and/or other in the real (uncontrollable) world. For Veronica, her most private of pleasures had been captured and was held in thrall by her invasive father. She sought men to excite and gratify in the hope that finally the right to her own pleasure would be returned to her. The other was always one more version of her internal kidnapper; the self she longed to set free could be only tem porarily released by her imagining or paying for surrogates.

The Slippery Slopes of Passion

We have been considering and reconsidering the common explanation of the degradation of romance as a consequence of the primitive nature of sexuality. If, as Yeats so powerfully put it in "Crazy Jane," "love has pitched his mansion in the place of excrement," romance is always precariously perched and in danger of slipping into the ooze, and we must perpetually seek firmer ground for a more stable abode. But if, as I have suggested, the very idea of sexuality as primitive is a product of our difficulty containing the various, contrasting facets of our experience of self in relation to others, this account needs revising.

If love and desire are difficult to sustain in the same relationship, it is not because they are generated from different phylogenetic levels. Love and desire are both thoroughly human. Our problem with them is that they orient us toward very different goals. Love seeks control, stability, continuity, certainty. Desire seeks surrender, adventure, novelty, the unknown. In love we are searching for points of attachment, anchoring, something we know we can count on. In desire we are searching both for missing, disowned pieces of ourselves and for something beyond ourselves, outside the borders of self-recognition that, under ordinary circumstances, we protect so fiercely.

Erotic passion destabilizes one's sense of self. When we find someone intensely arousing who makes possible unfamiliar experiences of ourselves and an otherness we find captivating, we are drawn into the disorienting loopiness of self/other. We tend to want to control these experiences and the others who inspire them. Thus emotional connection tends to degrade into strategies for false security that suffocate desire. And sexual excitement tends to degrade into those elements common to all (both abnormal and normal) perversions—collapsed expectations and omnipotence, which obliterate possibilities for love. Sustaining the unstable tensions of romance and regaining romantic states over time in the same relationship require a struggle to resist these inevitable efforts to draw moving but unsettling experiences under our control. In the dialectics of eroticism that constitute the strange loop of our sexuality, our journey into the otherness of the other often surprises us with unknown features of ourselves, and our exploration of our interiority, the ineffable privacy of the self, often surprises us with the presence of others.

3

Idealization, Fantasy, and Illusions

Inescapable romance, inescapable choice
Of dreams, disillusion as the last illusion,
Reality as a thing seen by the mind,
Not that which is but that which is apprehended
—WALLACE STEVENS

ONE OF THE FIRST PRINCIPLES of abnormal psychology I learned in my undergraduate days was conveyed in an easy-to-remember saying: neurotics daydream about sandcastles in the sky; psychotics live in them. This saying reflects three states of mind: the fantasy world of the neurotic, the delusional world of the psychotic, and a singular reality, solid and dependable, in which the speaker, the non-neurotic, non-psychotic, presumably lives. That was thirty years ago.

In the churning maelstrom of contemporary life, these realms are no longer distinct and separable. We are working out new and more complex realities on every level of cultural life—from the virtual reality of computer chat rooms and multi-user domains, to cartoon characters like the Simpsons or the diminutive cynics of South Park who sometimes seem to cut to a clearer truth, to the often night-marish worlds of punk and MTV, to the epistemological revolutions of hermeneutics, constructivism, and postmodernism. What are we to make of fantasy, delusion, and reality now? How are we to understand their place in our emotional lives, both normal and psychopathological?

If sexuality generates the energy that drives romantic passion, idealization provides the compass, organizing and orienting our devotion. A crucial ingredient of the rapture of romance is the sense that the object of desire is no ordinary person but someone very special, someone unique. There is a certain magic to romance, according to the common lore of love, a spell, that infatuates, that transforms mundane, expectable reality into something transcendent, a kind of personal domain of the sacred. Romance is an altered state of consciousness; in our Disney-created idiom, it turns the monochromatic into Technicolor.

Thus, the centrality of idealization in romantic love, the source of its magic, is also one important cause of its fragility. Ideals are easily tarnished, spells broken, sleights of hand exposed. After their one rapturous night together, Romeo and Juliet dread the light. (Juliet desperately mistakes the song of the morning lark for that of the nightingale.) If romance is contingent upon the illusions of idealization, it can only be fleeting or seriously deluded. In our popular wisdom, the intense idealization that is central to "falling in love" is regressive and childlike, laced with fantasy. Romance fades over time because familiarity provides a more realistic, "warts and all" view of the other; the harsh sunlight of the morning after dispels the enchantment of the moonlight. The most we can hope for is that infatuation will be transformed into a more sober "liking."

Cathy, a woman in her forties who had been married for twelve years, realized that she still felt a brief "thrill" when, at the end of the day, she saw her husband, with whom she lived in a state of measured distance and chronic grievance. It made her uncomfortable to notice that thrill, which she had been happy to feel in the early months of their relationship. There had been several crushing disappointments over the years with him. Cathy had had a history of early trauma and abandonment, and she had also felt, at times, betrayed and abandoned by her husband. She was ambivalent about this newly recovered excitement. The thrill, she believed, was connected with her early fantasies about her husband, which she had come to regard as benighted and unrealistic. She was wiser than that now. She felt that allowing herself to stay with and cultivate the thrill might lead her to soften her internal stance toward her husband, which would amount to forgiving him for the disappointments of the past and renouncing claims to reparations and guarantees in the future. She wasn't prepared to do either.

Cathy's love, like romance in general, was sparked by her idealization. Her husband had seemed unique, but he turned out to be all too common. What is the origin of such romantic fantasies? How can convictions of uniqueness possibly stand the test of time?

Narcissism and Idealization for Freud

Freud's elucidation of romance and idealization, with his characteristic incisiveness, provides a window into the inner logic, the presuppositions, of the common understanding of the nature of romantic love. Freud defines idealization as "overvaluation." Things are what they are; they have a certain objective value. When we idealize something—another person, a quality in ourselves, an idea or a cause—we attribute to it an illusory value, beyond the value to which it is legitimately entitled. Idealization can cover a lot of ground, from a worshipful, self-abnegating deference, surely self-destructive, to the experience of being "head over heels" about another person.

Where does this tendency toward overvaluation come from? Freud saw its origins in the infantile state of mind of the newborn. He imagined the infant with no rational capacities, no ability to differentiate inside from outside, self from other, bathed in a kind of self-satisfied libidinal glow. The world is pleasurable, and the world is me. Freud termed this first psychological state "primary narcissism," after the self-enamored Narcissus of Greek myth. Gradually the infant's attention is redirected outward, toward others, on whom he depends for his pleasures and survival. His primary narcissism gets broken up and dispersed. He overvalues the providers of his pleasures, as primary narcissism is redirected and transformed into what Freud called "object-love." But our narcissistic self-love serves always as a foil to, a ready retreat from, the vicissitudes of our dealings with others: Who can possibly love us as well and as dependably as we love ourselves?

Yet overvaluation is precarious no matter where it is aimed. Remember what happened to Narcissus; he disappeared into the dark waters beneath the illusion of his own reflection. Narcissism, in Freud's outlook, is very dangerous. What happened to Narcissus can happen to you and me. Too much narcissism, excessive idealization of self, draws one away from the real world and results in madness. But too much externalization of one's pool of narcissism into another, in a romantic idealization of someone else, is also dangerous. Romantic longing depletes the self; all value is located in the other. Romantic obsession, Freud believed, is the inverse of psychosis; unrequited love, narcissistic expenditures with no return, can lead to self-loathing and suicide.

Most often the idealization of self or other leads to neither madness nor suicidal despair. The instability generated by the overvaluation of romance is, under the best of circumstances, replaced in fairly short order, and with a sigh of relief, by a more stable, rational perspective. In psychological health, the other, like the self, comes to be valued appropriately. The spell is broken; the illusions of infatuation are dispersed and replaced by a sober, more real perspective.

It has been noted, by Erich Fromm and others, that Freud's vision of life, emerging in the context of late-nineteenth-century European culture, reflected both Romantic and Enlightenment currents. A Romantic sensibility is unmistakable in Freud's theory of the instincts and the unconscious: we are driven by dark, unknown forces. Yet the Romantic strain in Freud was always thoroughly tempered by a deep commitment to Enlightenment rationality: there is a correct, rational, scientific, fantasy-free way to understand the world. The fantasy-driven illusions of the pleasure principle can and should be replaced, through hard work and discipline, by the objective understanding of the reality principle. Freud's profound commitment to the Enlightenment ideal of objective rationality is nowhere more apparent than in his thinking about love. Romance is transitory because the idealization upon which it is based is not real. Departures from reality, from rational evaluations of either self or other, are dangerous. Our stability depends on accurate valuation.

From our current historical vantage point, there is a striking irony to Freud's devotion to science. Freud's life coincided with the late-nineteenth-, early-twentieth-century triumph of science, not just in its technological, practical applications, but as a worldview. Freud, like most of the progressive intellectuals of his day, regarded science as a methodology that allowed human beings to see, grasp, and manipulate the world. According to the wisdom of Freud's time, the prior reigning worldview of Western culture, the Judeo-Christian tradition, had enshrouded reality with fantasies, myths, and illusions. Science, Freud and his contemporaries believed, clears away the fog and mystification, allowing us to see the world objectively, as it really is. Telescopes bring the distant heavens within view; microscopes give us access to the miniature, the subvisual; X-rays allow us to see inside of things; and the psychoanalytic method grants us access to the inner, unconscious workings of the human mind. It is no wonder that there was a widespread belief in the early decades of the twentieth century that science would set us on the right path for solving all our problems. Hard-headed, rational thought would prove our guide to understanding not only material reality but ethics and politics as well. With a vision cleared of frills and fantasies, we could assign appropriate, objective value to things. Thus, for Freud and his contemporaries, science generated scientism, a devotion to an objectivism that was believed to have been stripped of wishes, illusions, and all the subjectivist vestiges of religion.

As we now know, things did not work out that way. The terrifying brinksmanship that was spawned by the development of nuclear energy and the ecological disasters that have accompanied technological advances have made us very aware of the difference between the capacity to understand and manipulate the material world and the wisdom to use that capacity wisely. And where shall that wisdom be found? For many today, the naked rationality of scientism in itself no longer seems sufficient. Although there has not been a broad return to traditional religion as a deeply guiding presence in human life, spirituality has certainly made something of a comeback, in the broad spectrum of activities, from yoga to New Age crystals, from meditation to family genealogies, that point beyond everyday, mundane reality to something deeper, something transcendent. From our perspective, the scientism of our early- and mid-twentieth-century predecessors seems less an expression of rationality than of faith. And Freud's belief that love relations could, and usefully should, be stripped of ideals, so that intimate others could be valued objectively and appropriately, is itself an extraordinary and highly improbable ideal—disillusion, as Wallace Stevens points out, "as the last illusion."

Nevertheless, our common wisdom on romantic love shares the basic assumptions to which Freud's objectivism led him. We seem to believe that other people are knowable in the same way as are natural objects, and that knowledge and proper valuation of the other accrue over time. We tend to think of the passion of romance as a state of illusory valuation, of intoxication. Fantasy, we are told, exploits the unfamiliar to construct ideals that, with the clearer vision time provides, can only fade.

The Family and the Emergence of Uniqueness

There is no better place to gain perspective on our own cultural assumptions, to grasp the social construction of experiences we unthinkingly regard as universal, than in the often surprising clash between our presuppositions and those of other cultures. Nathaniel Branden tells a story about Dr. Audrey Richards, an anthropologist who worked with the Bemba of Northern Rhodesia in the 1930s. Dr. Richards, he says, once told a group of the Bemba "an English folk-fable about a young prince who climbed glass mountains, crossed chasms, and fought dragons, all to obtain the hand of a maiden he loved. The Bemba were plainly bewildered, but remained silent. Finally an old chief spoke up, voicing the feelings of all present in the simplest of questions: 'Why not take another girl?' he asked."

The sense of uniqueness is the centerpiece of romantic passion in Western culture. There is no one else like the beloved, the lover believes: "We were made for each other." It might seem merely coincidental that the sense of uniqueness essential to romantic love is also found in the other relationship that is a recurrent source of meaning in contemporary life—the love of parents for their children. But this is no accident. The romance of passionate love and the romance of parental love, along with the romance of self-love, all evolved together in the shift from medieval society to modern family life. A consideration of their common origins sheds some light on the developmental precursors of romantic passion and the delicacy of its inner structure.

According to some historians, the very concepts of the "family" and "childhood" were nonexistent in the Middle Ages and emerged during the enormous social, economic, and political changes that transformed Europe between the fifteenth and seventeenth centuries. This seems a little puzzling. Of course there were families and children throughout human history and prehistory, and it is difficult for us not to imagine that people have always structured and experienced their familial relationships in the same ways we do now. But the deep sense of individualism that fueled modern Western culture, and the sharp divide between public and private realms that is crucial to the modern family, are relatively recent innovations.

In earlier times, marriages served the purpose of reproduction, the transmission of life, property, and lineage. And what we today regard as the precious and enormously eventful stage of life we call "childhood" was regarded almost as a larval pre-stage of life, the way most people today regard fetal life. The high incidence of infant mortality made it difficult to take small children seriously until they reached an age (around seven, at the conclusion of a long weaning) that established their viability. Before that age, they were generally sent out of the home (for wetnursing) and not yet considered as part of society. We tend to react with horror to the callousness of the Roman and traditional Chinese practices of murderous exposure of unwanted newborns. But these practices had a common source with the indifference of medieval culture toward its newborns: it was only after surviving several years that a baby became a person. Only as hygienic procedures dramatically reduced infant mortality was childhood discovered as an interesting and compelling stage of life; only then did parents' emotional attachment to their children begin to play a central part in their lives. Before that, as Phillipe Ariès puts it, "the general feeling was . . . that one had several children in order to keep just a few. People could not allow themselves to become too attached to something that was regarded as a probable loss." "The little one did not count because she could disappear." But little ones began to count, and that had a profound impact on the structure of contemporary emotional life.

Romantic passion has existed as a potential throughout human history, and we find stories of romantic love in the Bible and other literature of antiquity. But these were exceptions, myths, experiences of gods and goddesses, kings and queens. Romance as an option, an expectation, for ordinary people living more or less ordinary lives appeared only with the emergence of the modern family, with the creation of the idea that children were something special and one's own children the most special of all. Thus it is no accident that the sense of uniqueness central to romantic love finds its counterpart in the love affair between parents and children. In his appropriation of the Oedipus myth, Freud attributed this love to the instinctually driven mind of the child. But many post-Freudian psychoanalytic authors have noted that Sophocles' story did not begin with Oedipus the lover and murderer but with the murderous abandonment of the infant Oedipus by Laius and Jocasta, his parents. And contemporary theorists have come to understand the pathology of adult love relations in terms of the vicissitudes of early family romances.

One of the central projects of psychotherapy as a field, and one of the basic challenges for each particular patient/therapist pair, is the exploration of the complex relationship between love and passion in adulthood and love and passion in childhood relations with parents.

Psychoanalysts daily encounter the problematic residues of parental love: either too much involvement and stimulation, the invasion of boundaries, the overwhelming of the immature self, or, alternatively, too little involvement, abandonment, an absence of the attention required by the immature self to come to life. Both overstimulation and understimulation result in serious difficulties in living. Because clinicians see the problems and can easily trace them back to developmental causes, they tend to imagine a healthy child-parent love that would only facilitate adult love and leave no problems. But it may be that childhood love is always fraught with areas of overstimulation and areas of understimulation, too much in some ways and too little in others. It may be that "just right" is found only in fairy tales.

Ideals and Romanticism

Romanticism developed as an alternative to the rationalist Western tradition that had culminated in the Enlightenment of the late seventeenth and early eighteenth centuries. According to Isaiah Berlin, the Enlightenment worldview was based on the following three principles: all genuine questions have true answers; all true answers are discoverable and teachable to others; and all the answers are in principle compatible, "or combinable into one harmonious whole like a jigsaw puzzle." Romanticism is grounded in a precisely opposite set of beliefs: there is no structure to things; we mold things according to our will; and they come into being only as a result of our molding activity. This antithetical epistemological foundation led to the array of different qualities and emphases associated with Romanticism: feelings, passions, ideals, creativity, and the imagination.

It is possible to paint, in very broad strokes, the dialectical swings between (Enlightenment) rationalism and Romanticism over the past several hundred years. Harold Bloom, for example, derives the turn inward of English Romantic poetry from disillusionment in the belief in a rational reordering of the external world:

> The background of English Romantic poetry of the first generation is the violent desire and subsequent disillusion associated with the French Revolution. Blake and Wordsworth, in different but parallel ways, transferred their hopes for men to a hope for the individual man, a man at the center of men who, by renovating himself, might begin on a more certain basis what had failed in the world of social and political movements. The poetry of Blake and of Wordsworth thus follows the lead of their great original, Milton, who also turned in his major works from the desire to see all things new in England to the search for a Paradise within.

The Romantic poets turned from pragmatic, political projects in the conventional world of consensual reality to a visionary world, from perception to imagination.

Is the visionary retreating from a failed reality into fantasy? Or is the visionary seeking out a more fundamental reality? Does Romanticism offer an escape from the "real" world (grasped by Enlightenment rationality) into an unreal, illusory world? Or does Romanticism provide an opening into a deeper experience, the more "real" underpinnings of experience? Some Romantic visionaries believed they had passed through the "doors of perception," in the words of the poet William Blake that were borrowed first by Aldous Huxley and later by the sixties rock group The Doors.

In traditional psychoanalytic parlance, with its Enlightenment commitments, Freud described the visionary, fantasy-driven imagination as a regression from secondary process to primary process, from rational valuation to overvaluation. This rationalistic tilt in Freud and traditional psychoanalytic thought reflects the collapse of the Romantic sensibility in the last decades of the nineteenth century, overwhelmed by the enthusiasm for science spawned by its staggering technological achievements. Nevertheless, with the waning of confidence that science itself will generate wisdom, the last several decades have witnessed a partial swing back toward a Romantic sensibility, in movements like existentialism, spiritualism, postmodernism, and poststructuralism, with all their offshoots. The common thread running through all these movements is a belief that rationality and objectivity, although good and useful for many purposes, may not be the exclusive or even the best route to engaging our world. This has particular relevance for the question of what brings another person alive for us as an object of love and desire.

The Imaginative Constructions of Desire

Imagination is the handmaiden of desire. What makes someone desirable is idealization, an act of imagination that highlights the qualities that make that person unique, special, out of the ordinary. The thrill Cathy could still discern in her response to her husband required such selectivity. Traditional epistemology, of professional philosophers, popular culture, and folk psychology, presumed the possibility of a purely objective take on reality, on others, on oneself. For someone to become an object of desire requires an imaginative transformation, in which perception is spiced by the illusions of fantasy to create a sweeter offering. In this understanding, the objective baseline is provided by perception, a passive rendering of the way *things really are*. Idealizations are all products of artificial sweeteners.

Many of the conceptual pillars of this traditional view have been slowly but decisively eroding. Psychologists have discovered that perception itself is not a passive but an active process; we need to learn to assemble discrete points of sensation into images that have meaning for us. Many epistemologists have come to regard objectivism itself as an impossible ideal, a longing for an unreachable epistemological "foundational" security. Many philosophers of science have discovered that the history of science is not a progressive, incremental approach to the truth, but rather a series of discontinuous paradigms for explaining and exploring different sorts of problems. And psychoanalysts have begun to think about fantasy not as hallucinatory, wish-fulfilling illusions that contaminate objective perception, but rather as the vehicle through which the world comes to life for each of us in a personal, vibrant fashion.

The concept of "reality-testing" has been the centerpiece of traditional psychological and psychoanalytic understandings of the nature and function of fantasy and the imagination. In the customary view, perceptions of the world around us, including other people, are influenced both by the way things really are and by our imaginative elaborations of the ways things are and our fantasies of how we would like things to be. Imagination and fantasy are potential contaminants, because they threaten to obscure our direct perception of how things really are. They are fine in their own domain, clearly identified as illusions, but the labels need to be kept very clear. Sandcastles are not habitable.

But recent theorists have begun to challenge the neat separation between our perceptions of how things really are and our fantasy-driven imagination. It may be, it is now believed, that we can only find a satisfying habitable dwelling by first identifying it as a favorite sandcastle.

Consider this startling definition of reality testing offered by Hans Loewald, the visionary American psychoanalyst: "Reality testing is far more than an intellectual or cognitive function. It may be understood more comprehensively as the experiential testing of fantasy—its potential and suitability for actualization—and the testing of actuality—its potential for encompassing it in, and penetrating it with, one's fantasy life. We deal with the task of a reciprocal transposition." Here reality is tested not to eliminate from it unrealistic infantile fantasies, but to probe it for sites in which one can locate and cultivate fantasies. For Loewald, the rational, objective perspective we normally consider "reality" is useful for many activities we require for adaptive living. But as a steady fare, objective reality becomes a devitalized shadow of a fuller experience that is made possible when the actual can be animated and brought alive through fantasy.

Whereas Freud saw fantasy as opposed to and clouding reality, major post-Freudian psychoanalytic authors regard fantasy as enriching and enhancing reality. Some perceptions of things, others, oneself treat the objects of perception for utilitarian purposes of one sort or another. In other approaches to things, others, oneself, objects of perception become objects of desire, and one constructs them differently, highlighting different features, exploring different facets, probing them, as Loewald suggests, for correspondence with one's own fantasies and longings.

The philosopher Elaine Scarry has recently explored some of these issues in our experience of beauty. We apprehend a beautiful thing, Scarry notes, outside its customary context, where it opens up into infinite possibilities: "the perceiver is led to a more capacious regard for the world." The philosopher Stuart Hampshire elaborates Scarry's theory: "There exists an unavoidable contrast between, on the one hand, the imaginative realm of objectively beautiful persons—persons with objectively beautiful faces, for example—and beautiful things, isolated and framed in our minds and, on the other, the confused realm of persons and things which we evaluate for their utility and their connections with other things."

The experience of beauty, Scarry is suggesting, entails a transcendence of ordinary reality. We tend to assume that ordinary reality is factual and objective, which makes the transcendence that transforms the ordinary other into an object of desire a fantasy-driven illusion. But if ordinary reality no longer wears the mantle of objectivity, if ordinary reality is understood as a construction, useful for some purposes, useless for others, its transcendence in the creation of the desirable is not a contamination or masking of *what is really there*, but an alternative construction, a window into *what is really there*.

The result of these profound shifts in the ways in which we understand our experience of things, others, and ourselves is not, as some fear, an inevitable relativism or solipsism, with all takes on reality equally valid and equally meaningless. The result is a more complex understanding of things, others, and ourselves, as offering many facets and considerable ambiguity, coming alive always, necessarily, partially through acts of imagination. Emotions, passions, desires are necessarily brought to experience to shape it in some way for us. Objectivity is a particular kind of passion, a thirst for disillusionment, which, as most obsessional neurotics eventually discover along with Stevens, is the "last illusion."

The Knowledge of Selves

Socrates enjoined us to "Know thyself," and the pursuit of self-knowledge has been a lodestar of Western philosophy and psychology for twenty-five hundred years. But what does it mean to know oneself? For Socrates and Plato, self-knowledge entailed the cultivation of a highly rarefied rationality unblemished by input from the senses. And as Judeo-Christian religiosity entered Western consciousness, self-knowledge entailed the sorting out of the sacred from the profane within one's own experience. Within these major currents of Western thought, self-love was always dangerous. Self-love draws one away from and clouds one's experience of what is truly important: a rational consideration of the nature of reality, or an appreciation of the divine.

Freud inherited this tradition, and he too considered excessive self-regard particularly dangerous. As noted earlier, Freud drew on his customary Greek sources and called self-love narcissism. Too much of it resulted in what he took to be the global self-absorption of schizophrenia, and a less total dose led to that most malignant of character pathologies, "narcissistic character disorder." Patients whom psychoanalysts fail to help are often labeled with this diagnosis and condemned by the judgment "unanalyzable." On the healthier end of the continuum, as well, narcissism was associated with infantilism, which, in more subtle ways, is a regressive element, an immaturity in a system measured according to rationality and the overcoming of egocentricity.

There has been a fundamental shift from classical Freudian psychoanalysis to contemporary psychoanalysis concerning these issues. Heinz Kohut, the founder of self psychology, introduced the concept of "healthy narcissism," formally an oxymoron but now referring to a robust sense of self-regard as an essential ingredient in mental health. Taking oneself seriously, Kohut suggests, requires some modulated, childlike grandiosity, a self-expansiveness unencumbered by concern with criticisms and other points of view, without fear of deflation. Healthy self-experience requires a certain episodic idealization of the self, a romancing of the self, as a source of vitality and creativity.

Freud considered scientists the prototype of health; they had learned to regulate and sublimate their infantile sexual and aggressive experience, harnessing its energies in the service of rationality and scientific exploration. Although Freud loved art and literature, he was always suspicious of artists, whose experience seemed closer to the fantasy life of the child. (Perhaps they seemed to be having too much fun.) It is a hallmark of the shift in basic psychoanalytic sensibility that the prototype of mental health for many contemporary analytic authors is not the scientist but the artist. A continual objective take on reality is regarded as neither possible nor valuable in contrast to the ability to develop and move in and out of different perspectives on reality. The ideal of self-deferential absorption in the study of external reality has been replaced by the ideal of self-expression and self-exploration. The injunction "Know thyself" has been amended by the injunctions "Express thyself" and "Explore thyself."

In some sense, this shift in what it means to know something also parallels changes in science itself from Freud's time to ours. The central implication of the "uncertainty principle" developed by the physicist Werner Heisenberg is that one cannot ascertain and describe both the velocity and the position of an electron at the same time. To determine its velocity is to change its position. To determine its position is to alter its velocity. Learning about something in the external world requires interacting with it, and that interaction has an impact on, changes, the thing one is studying. This is certainly true of knowledge of selves, one's own or another's. What one discovers in another person depends a great deal on who one is and how one approaches the other. And what one learns about oneself depends a great deal upon how one approaches oneself and for what purposes.

What becomes of self-knowledge in this view? Is it healthy to be deluded about my own importance? My place in the universe? My significance to others? Of course not. What is healthy is the capacity to sustain multiple estimations of oneself, different ones for different purposes. In this view, an inability to recognize one's shortcomings can be an obstacle to meaningful, mutual exchanges with others.

At the same time, a preoccupation with one's shortcomings and an inability to romance one's self can serve as a defense against allowing oneself to become excited about one's potential and engage others in a robust fashion. Knowing oneself is a complicated business, because knowing one version of oneself can be a defense against knowing and being surprised by other versions of oneself. Thus, in contemporary psychoanalytic terms, knowing oneself is much less a goal to be achieved than a process to be immersed in.

The fundamental shifts in our understanding of the ways in which we construct our realities have an important bearing on how we understand what we mean when we say we *know* another person. We can know another in many different ways: for all sorts of utilitarian purposes, and also as an object of beauty, which requires a highlighting of facets that are not emphasized in everyday contexts. There is no good reason to assume, that the other is any less conflictual, any less multiplicitous, any less contextual than oneself. And there is no good reason to assume, either, that the everyday construction of the other is any more or less real than the transcendent, idealized construction of the other as an object of desire. The conviction that we really *know* the other, in a dependable, predictable, certain fashion, is a dangerous illusion.

Yet there is a good reason to want to believe we really know others in a predictable way. We depend on and desire them to a degree that can sometimes be frightening. So we are perpetually drawn to construct them in more stable, knowable terms, as ordinary and flawed rather than as extraordinary and flawless.

The even-keeled, quotidian response to a partner may be adaptive over time because it keeps passion and therefore disappointment and anger at a minimum. But deciding whether it is more realistic or not is complicated. Sometimes it is based on a selective repression of the very real, desirable qualities that ignited passion originally. Once again, idealization appears to be good for some things and bad for others.

Idealization and Its Hazards

Consider this description, drawn from the psychoanalytic literature, of the sadomasochistic experience of the sexual pervert:

> This fantasy of part-objects manipulated without loss unfolds in a world that the sadomasochist has split off or dissociated, in an altered state of consciousness characterized by extreme sexual excitement, sharply diminished reflective self-awareness, and a diminished sense that his acts are his own and under voluntary control. While in this altered state he feels as if hypnotized or in an *erotic haze,* and under its spell events take on a hyperreal and hallucinatory quality that makes them seem larger and more compelling than reality itself. What I call the erotic haze serves to deny that reality is not in accord with fantasy.

I must admit, even though I don't consider my own interpersonal relations especially sadomasochistic, this erotic haze sounds pretty good to me. Extreme sexual excitement, diminished reflective self-awareness, a reduced experience of willful control, a sense of hyper-reality: sign me up! Are these not important features of the rapture of being in love, of enthrallment? Of course, the author of the quoted passage is concerned with these experiences as they occur not in a mutually loving relationship but in perversions, where the rapture is carefully orchestrated and controlled and the other is captive. The problem is the absense of any bridge between reality and the fantasy that makes such rapture possible.

Does the lack of accord between everyday reality and idealizing fantasies that generate rapturous passion suggest that the former is

more "real" and the latter are perverse, dangerous illusions inimical to a stable long-term relationship? Or might we regard idealization as, sometimes, a process of bringing alive features of the other
that are hidden and masked in ordinary, everyday interactions?
Might we regard idealizing passion as the Romantics regarded
visionary imagination and as Scarry regards the appreciation of
beauty, as an act that transcends the utilitarian pragmatics of everyday living by allowing us access to something more real, less
detached, less (not more) manipulative?

If we regard everyday reality as an objective baseline, a no-frills,
unadorned truth, then the idealizing imagination is an illusion
machine. But if we regard everyday reality as a construction of our
world, others, and ourselves—essential for many of our purposes,
but only one among many possible constructions—then the idealizing imagination may sometimes, not always, bring out and
respond to facets of our world, others, and ourselves that are quite
real but ordinarily occluded by other concerns.

Long-term relationships, particularly those entailing creating a
home, raising children, sharing housekeeping, and owning real
estate, are necessarily utilitarian: if they are to last, they have to
work. In these relationships the weaknesses and vulnerabilities of
the two partners are often salient: the less you do and can do, the
more I have to do and the less I can depend on you. We crave safety,
stability, predictability, and rightly so; our emotional equanimity
depends upon it. But idealization destabilizes and draws things out
of their ordinary, everyday priorities and perspectives. The idealizing imagination is, by its very nature, unsafe, and we tend to find
ways of trying to practice damage control by managing and segregating it.

The argument that the no-frills, pragmatic approach to life and
relationships is not necessarily any more "real" than idealized

accounts does not suggest that all idealizations are equally compelling, that anything our imagination cooks up is a useful basis for
romantic passion. Idealizations, like all views, are highly selective,
but some idealizations are truer to their inspiration than others. It
matters a great deal whether the source of idealization is at least
partially in the other (highlighted and elaborated through imagination) or purely a figment of the fantasy life of the lover, exploit-
ing the other as an occasion for the projection of his or her own
needs. Adoring a lover for his or her (not always dependable) beauty
or wit or kindness is likely to be more serviceable over time than
adoring a lover for his or her ability to fly or predict the future!
Thus it may be useful to distinguish between ideals and pseudo-
ideals in love.

And the serviceability of idealization in romantic relationships
also depends on the extent to which idealizing narratives are developed as co-constructed, collaborative activities. A lover's idealization tends to be more fertile when the qualities chosen correspond
to ways in which the beloved enjoys idealizing herself. Often mutual
idealization extends to a joint enjoyment of a partial mythology for
two: "We were made for each other." In some sense, there is some
truth to this sentiment, as both participants in a significant relationship shape themselves over time in the context of their intimacy
with the other, making themselves partially for each other. But
fantasies of perfect harmony and synchrony can be enormously
destructive if taken too seriously, as a steady expectation, rather
than as a transient, episodic connection.

Our longing for safety and our thirst for passion pull us in opposite directions. As Freud noted long ago, all idealizing excitement
places the lover in a dangerous state. The excitement may not be
reciprocated; love may remain unrequited. It is bad enough at the
beginning of a relationship, with someone you do not know well;

there is so much less at stake. But falling into an intense, passionate idealization of someone you count on for safety and predictability is hazardous indeed. That person knows *you* too well, with all your flaws and blemishes. There is too much at stake.

From this perspective, the common experience of the fading of romance over time may have less to do with the inevitable under-cutting of idealization by reality and familiarity than with the increasing danger of allowing oneself episodic, passionate idealization in a relationship that one depends on for security and predictability. Intense excitement about another is a dangerous business; it often is much safer to surrender to it with a person one cannot possibly spend much time with or will never see again. Sustaining desire for something important from someone important is the central danger of emotional life. What is so dangerous about desiring someone you have is that you can lose him or her. Desire for someone unknown and unobtainable operates as a defense against desire for someone known and obtainable, therefore capable of being lost.

Idealization does not necessarily dissipate in relationships, but new perspectives are added, and some are inevitably disappointing. It is not that romance necessarily fades over time, but it does become riskier. Love is sometimes described as "being crazy" about another person. To be crazy about someone you actually depend on for a variety of security needs, real and illusory, can feel crazed indeed. Thus, like Cathy, the partners in many couples come to inhibit the appreciation and excitement they felt about each other earlier in the relationship. They tell themselves they know the other better now. What they know now is that the features they once idealized in the other are not *all* there is to the other, that the other is also disappointing, and therefore that their passion cannot be a steady state. So they use what they know of the other as a defense against the surrender of idealization. The adored features of the other may not have been illusory at all; what was illusory was the guarantee they sought against disappointment and perpetually regenerated solitude. The deepening of dependency and the inevitability of episodic disappointment makes idealized perspectives and the excitement they arouse more dangerous, because they are not the whole story. Surrender to romantic imagination is warded off by a sober, selective clinging to frailties so that excitement can be controlled.

We are probably all thrill-seekers in one way or another, but thrills are risky. So we tend to try to keep the thrills controlled and predictable, as with a roller coaster that stays on the tracks. Some seek cheap thrills in fleeting or completely controllable relationships in which the stakes are always low. And the ever-intensifying fascination with celebrities seems to feed our hunger for idealization and our fear of its consequences by glorifying and then exposing and destroying our "stars."

Carl sought psychoanalytic therapy because his relationship with his wife of many years had become sparse and dull. He was an artist of considerable renown and had been greatly absorbed in his work at the expense of his marriage. He felt he still loved his wife, but he was at a loss as to how they might rekindle the passion of their first intimacies. Carl began to explore memories of their early years together which were very exciting and passionate. As he spoke of their romance, his eyes would fill with tears at the thought of what a remarkable woman his wife had been and still was. Although he was able to tell me about his intense memories and secret, continuing admiration for her, Carl felt it would not be possible for him to tell her. To speak to her about his appreciation, past and present, felt to him like a form of pandering. To romance her, as it were, would be to put himself in the position of asking for something, perhaps begging. To allow himself to crave her would make him seem craven to her and himself. He had come to feel that his stalwart performance as husband had earned him the right to her love. To approach her appreciatively or seductively would be to renounce those claims.

There was a long family history around Carl's anti-romantic worldview. His father had been a high-ranking Marine officer whose career had been cut short because he believed his advancement should have been secured by his achievements on the field of battle, with no need to pay his dues through administrative and social participation at the Pentagon. He felt, as George and I came to talk of it, above "romancing" his superiors. Thus, for Carl, desire had become synonymous with begging and humiliation, appreciation synonymous with a self-demeaning pandering. The only love worth having was earned through virtuous deeds. The anti-erotic fallout of that worldview became increasingly apparent to Carl.

Fantasy and Eroticism

Passion arises in the tension between reality and fantasy. If it is dangerous to fantasize about what one feels one *has* in reality, or needs to believe one has, it is safer to fantasize about what one does *not* have. What makes fantasies of sex with someone unavailable or inaccessible, fantasies of sex with the mysterious stranger, so compelling? Their allure is not simply that they provide an opportunity to explore the forbidden and precarious; they also provide an opportunity to fantasize about the forbidden and precarious in a safer venue than do actual relationships. Anonymous fantasies allow an experience of danger under omnipotent control, like the roller coaster that dips and loops but never leaves the tracks. Safe thrills.

Erica Jong, in *Fear of Flying,* brilliantly captured the omnipotence of passionate imagination in her depiction of the "fantasy of the zipless fuck": "The zipless fuck was more than a fuck. It was a platonic ideal. Zipless because when you came together zippers fell away like rose petals, underwear blew off in one breath like dandelion fluff. Tongues intertwined and turned liquid. Your whole soul flowed out through your tongue and into the mouth of your lover." For the zipless fuck to retain its passion, Jong's narrator explains, it is essential "never to know the man very well." Brevity is good, anonymity even better. No talking at all is best:

> The zipless fuck is absolutely pure. It is free of ulterior motives. There is no power game. The man is not "taking" and the woman is not "giving." No one is attempting to cuckold a husband or humiliate a wife. No one is trying to prove anything or get anything out of anyone. The zipless fuck is the purest thing there is. And it is rarer than the unicorn. And I have never had one. Whenever it seemed I was close, I discovered a horse with a papiermâché horn, or two clowns in a unicorn suit.

Actual relationships, as Jong's narrator finds out, are always entangled with ulterior motives and power games. But this does not mean that passionate fantasies, like unicorns, are useless. It means that whether they are enriching or depleting depends on the way they are positioned in relation to actuality. Do they encourage an episodic selectivity and elaboration of the beauty of the partner? Or do they foster the illusion that there are other potential partners in the world who are only beautiful and never disappointing?

Idealization is destabilizing: it shifts our values, our priorities, our purposes; it undermines the utilitarian approach to practical realities that our lives require most of the time. "Falling" is not a viable way of life, and so we tell ourselves that the transition from "falling in love" to "being in love" or a more sober "liking" represents a dispelling of fantasy, a landing on solid ground. We try to keep our footing sure by degrading idealization into mere intoxicating illusion; we are wiser and know better now. However, it is not at all clear that the solid ground we perpetually seek is any more real than the idealizations that inspire passion. It is, rather, selected for different purposes.

4

Aggression and the Danger of Desire

———

To live in anger is to forget that one was ever weak, to
believe that what others call weakness is a sham, a
feint that one exposes and removes, like the sanitizing
immolation of a plague-ridden house.

—MARY GORDON

WE TEND TO REGARD ROMANCE as an expression of the
best of us, our most tender, sweetest, most loving sentiments. That
is why it is often startling when romantic love turns instantly into its
opposite—hatred. Romance, like politics, makes for strange bedfellows. The bedfellows of romance are not always other ennobling,
inspiring feelings like devotion or admiration, but often expressions
of the worst of us, the darker side of human experience: envy, jealousy, hatred, and a deep malevolence. Romantic infatuation, we are
told, is most usefully mellowed into something less intense and
more stable. But the road from being *in* love to *loving* is no easy
route. Cliffs on either side plunge the would-be lover rapidly into
the most hateful feelings and actions of which we are capable.

Sometimes romantic passion turns into intense hatred and a thirst
for revenge which, in extreme form, motivate actual violent crimes.

But passionate hatred comes in many subtler forms, and everyday crimes against objects of desire are very much a part of ordinary life: emotional detachment, provocative testing, strategies of control, retaliation. The most interesting crimes of passion for most of us take place only in our minds. But our minds are very important places.

A recurrent theme in the popular wisdom on love is that romance is fragile because human beings are naturally aggressive: love's contamination by hatred is inevitable. It is natural enough to regard aggression and hatred as inimical to love, to try to protect love with a vigilant civility. But many lovers have experienced the profound relief at love's survival of the dreaded first real knock-down, drag-out fight. A love that has endured episodic aggression has a depth and resilience obtainable in no other way. Because of love's profound risks, hatred is its inevitable accompaniment, and, paradoxically, the survival of romance depends not on skill in avoiding aggression but on the capacity to contain it alongside love. We shall see that inhibitions in hating a potential object of desire can serve as an obstacle to the development of romantic passion.

A Secret Vengeance

Jake, a high-level corporate executive in his mid-forties, worked for a company that had originally been a family business founded by his maternal grandfather. His father, who had died suddenly in his fifties, had also worked for the company, but in a lesser position. His mother, her father's favorite child, was a powerful, matriarchal presence in both family and business matters, which often blurred together. Jake's relationships with women had been serially monogamous. They generally began with an intense romantic excitement that quickly dissipated, intimacy often turning into cordial friendship.

Jake was quite successful by most conventional standards. Yet he had trouble taking himself seriously, which was why he sought psychoanalytic treatment. He regarded himself as a boy posing as a man. He felt he had a privileged, wonderful, quite easy life, ensconced within his mother's powerful domain. Still, despite a job that was fairly demanding and entailed considerable responsibility, Jake lacked a sense of his own power, or even activity, in the world. A central feature of his sense of boyishness was his preferred sexual activity: surreptitious public masturbation.

Slowly, analytic inquiry revealed the pervasiveness of Jake's sense that in every other activity in his life besides masturbation he was under the control of others, doing their bidding, taking their direction, meeting their standards. The only thing he experienced himself as *really* wanting to do was to masturbate. This was the ultimate act of self-pleasure, pure self-affirmation. Sex with others has its charms, but one has to *deal* with them, and one's own pleasure, one's own self-assertion becomes subverted. So, over the years, Jake refined his masturbatory practices, in the way one might cultivate an aesthetic taste or an athletic performance. He lived in a constant struggle over how much time to devote to these pleasures. He made a wide range of commitments so that he was plagued with the sense that he was being kept from what he really wanted to do. Yet when he did devote himself to his preferred activity, he would begin to feel a growing sense of guilt and self-betrayal. He would feel he was wasting his time, being unmanly, indulging in something distinctly adolescent. This intense, irresolvable conflict had a great deal to do with his sense of posing, of not being a man among other men.

As analytic inquiry into the textures of Jake's experience became more fine-grained, we made some surprising discoveries. His quintessential sexual moment, which he had cultivated gradually over many years, worked as follows: Jake would sit in his car on a street in the downtown area of the small city where he lived, with a sport coat over his lap, stimulating himself. There was a great sense of adventure—as in a hunt—in the way he structured the experience. The goal was to visually capture an especially attractive, sexy woman passerby. He would keep himself in a state of arousal until just the right woman came along, who was exciting enough for him to stimulate himself to orgasm. It was important to find a spot on a street that was busy enough and fashionable enough to attract suitable prey. But it was dangerous to position himself in an area so busy that he might be detected. The sense of self-exposure was an important part of the thrill. There was a wonderful feeling connected to the idea that he was exposing himself in such close proximity to his unknowing victim, and the act was accompanied by a powerful, angry, "in your face" defiance. Yet he was horrified at the possibility that he might actually be discovered. He knew he could be arrested, which, he imagined, would destroy his family and his life.

Nested inside this carefully constructed experience was another delicately crafted tension between the public and the private, between desire and control. One might have thought that fantasy would be an important feature of Jake's adventures, that he would use the privacy of his own mind to imagine powerful sexual dominance over the prey he was silently stalking and using for his own secret purposes. But it had become very important to Jake *not* to imagine anything: no nakedness, no sexual acts. It was essential that there be no fantasied activity at all, only pure responsiveness to what he had found. Jake reacted to the visual impression of the woman as she presented herself on the street, and if she was attractive enough, arousing enough excitement in him, he would, finally, after what might be hours of preparatory buildup, allow himself to come. And at the moment of his orgasm he would find himself uttering not sounds of appreciation but expressions of contempt: "Filthy slut!" "Bitch!"

Jake organized the psychological expanse of his life to protect a secret domain, just for him, free of the deference to women that he felt his life so thoroughly required. Yet the activity in his carefully cultivated, solitary, defiant sexual pleasure mirrored the pervasive passivity, the submission to women, that characterized the rest of his life. Nested within this secret defiance was a further surrender to anonymous women whom he both captured and submitted to, accompanied by a deep, profound, hateful rage. The passion of his sexual activity, his devotional visual stalking of and surrender to women, had a great deal to do with this anger.

At the center of Jake's secret sexual life, his personal romance, were three powerful kinds of experiences: desire, dependency, and rage. What are the relationships among these feelings, this tight triad that fueled Jake's passion? Are aggression and hatred, like Jake's, toward objects of desire "natural" or pathological? Is aggression itself primary, in the way we think of love and desire as primary, or is it a consequence of deprivation and failure? Where does dependency come in? Are Jake's passive longings in relation to women a natural dimension of desire or an infantilization of desire? What is the relationship between a passive longing to be taken care of and a desire for mutuality and intimacy, between what seem like developmentally earlier and developmentally later dimensions of romance? These are not simple questions. Philosophers and psychologists have been struggling with various ways of answering them for many centuries.

Hawks and Doves

There are many ways to tell the story of human history, but surely any account of our past must include a chronicle of bloody violence, human against human. It seems that people have always brutalized one another, on a continuum from subtle psychological power plays to torture and genocide. Why is that? Where do aggression, rage, and hatred come from? There have been two basic approaches toward this question within our culture, and Freud gravitated to each of them, one after the other. Let's call the proponents of these theories of aggression the hawks and the doves.

The hawks believe that human beings are violent by nature, that we are fundamentally predatory, with a deep antipathy toward our own kind. There have been many versions of this position. Within the British political philosophy that has shaped our form of government, its most influential and articulate spokesperson was Thomas Hobbes. Human beings, left to their own devices, will butcher one another in short order, Hobbes suggested. The natural order is a state of chaos, of "war of everyone against everyone." Therefore we need laws to protect us from one another so that we can pursue our personal pleasures.

Within psychology, the ethologist Konrad Lorenz has provided the most forceful expression of the hawk position in recent years. We have evolved over the course of evolution to be territorial, fighting animals, Lorenz argued. Aggression emerges in our bodies as an adaptive, primary need, a relentless force, in a fashion analogous to hunger. It serves special survival needs: dividing the environment, ensuring a sexual advantage to the strongest, and providing a basis for the establishment of a leadership hierarchy. Aggression demands gratification. If no outlets for violence are available, belligerence leaks out around the edges of our personalities. If there are no wars to fight, we need competitive sports to divert aggression into benign channels. If we have no obvious enemies, we begin looking for a fight.

In contrast, the doves believe that human beings are social and loving by nature. Aggression does not bubble up from inside; it contaminates us from outside. There have also been many versions of this position. Within the continental political philosophy that provided an important counterpoint to British theorists like Hobbes and John Locke in shaping Western political and social structure, human beings are incomplete as individuals and require a community to become fully actualized. For Jean Jacques Rousseau, for example, the state of nature is one of harmony, since every human being has an "innate repugnance to see his fellow man suffer." According to the doves, the violence of human history has been generated by deprivation, corruption, and interference with what is naturally social and cooperative. Thus Rousseau locates the source of human violence in the contaminating influence of scarcity and private property: "War is a relationship between things, not men, which is to say that a state of war cannot arise out of mere personal relations; it arises, rather, out of property relations." In psychological theory, the most comprehensive development of this point of view was the American behaviorists' "frustration/aggression" hypothesis: aggression emerges in human experience in response to frustration. It has no independent motivational source; it arises when more loving, benign activities are thwarted.

Hawks and doves fly together. They almost seem to require each other. In psychoanalysis, for example, Freud initially flirted with a dovelike perspective but eventually came to embrace the concept of an innate aggressive drive that imparted a distinctly hawklike cast to traditional psychoanalysis. However, after Freud became a hawk, dovelike positions emerged in various neo-Freudian or post-Freudian schools. Human beings are not driven by an aggressive drive, it was argued; human beings seek attachment, interpersonal intimacy, or self-cohesion, and become aggressive only when these more fundamental motivations are thwarted.

It is not only academic philosophers and psychoanalytic clinicians who struggle with this controversy. We all do, in our own particular ways. A central feature of being a person, certainly in our time, is arriving at a sense of our personal nature: What are people like in general? What am I like? How one understands and experiences the roots of evil and cruelty, the darker passions, is a crucial element in the shaping of the personal self. In finding my own position on the origins of aggression, I am framing a view of my individual experience, establishing a version of my personal history, shaping the categories and tones of my inner life. What is the relationship between love and hate? What are people fundamentally after? What am I after? When things go wrong in my relationships, when love turns to hate, when tensions arise, how do I account for them? Where do I place myself within my own life-historical events? How do I understand my own motives, explain my own cruelties and betrayals? When romance turns into the blues, how do I tell the story of what has happened?

Through the eyes of the hawk, aggression is the inevitable expression of the lust for power and dominance. Wars, virulent nationalism, and social violence are inevitable; social stability can be maintained only through discipline and "law and order." On a personal level, intimacy is regarded warily, love as a transient state, a brief interlude within our more fundamental wariness toward one another; love, if we are lucky, is soon replaced by responsibility and respect. Of course things go wrong; what else can we expect? Relationships break down when our truer nature emerges.

Through the eyes of the dove, aggression is a response to frustration and deprivation. Wars, virulent nationalism, and social violence are results of prior trauma, poverty, and hopelessness; social stability can only be attained through cooperation, redistribution of resources, and equality. On a personal level, intimacy and love are regarded optimistically, as easy to establish and quite feasible to maintain. Relationships break down when we have been diverted from our truer nature, when we haven't been loving or loved enough.

I've sketched these positions in pared-down, pure terms. They are rarely found in quite such extreme form. Most of us oscillate between these perspectives on matters political and social, personal and interpersonal, shifting back and forth depending on our life experience. One reason for the flux is that the vantage points of both the hawk and the dove are compelling in certain ways, yet neither is wholly satisfying.

Part of what makes the hawk's vision persuasive is that aggression, hatred, and rage all *seem* so biologically grounded and fundamental. They generate and, at the same time, are expressions of specific bodily states of great emotional and physical intensity. Our bodies change when we become angry: our pulse races, our hormones surge, our physical strength seems to intensify. Aggression, through competitiveness and revenge, is unquestionably a powerful motivator of much of human experience. We are animals, hawk rhetoric tells us, and we can survive only by coming to terms with our primitive, dark side, which perpetually pulls us toward violence.

Yet for many of us there is something *too* dark about the hawk's perspective. We are animals, to be sure. But it is difficult to think of another animal as violent as human beings. And in most human experience aggression does not seem so random and relentless as the notion of an aggressive instinct suggests. Aggression is not a continuous, internally arising pressure, the way, for example, hunger is; aggression appears to be more episodic and situational. Consider the social relations of our close relatives the bonobo, among whom aggression is surely not unknown, but who do not appear to be driven by aggression as a propulsive force: "Living in a relatively nonviolent, egalitarian, and female-centered society, the bonobo may have much to offer in this regard." In the culture of the bonobo, there seems to be some precipitant for most violence, a threat, a trauma, an insult, something that feels endangering, real or imagined, that sets it off.

Consider the most persistent political violence in our time: between the Moslems and Serbs in Bosnia, the Catholics and Protestants in Northern Ireland, the Israelis and the Palestinians, the Hutus and the Tutsis in Rwanda. The worst aggression does not just erupt, now here, now there, in a random fashion; it is part of a cyclical pattern of trauma, endangerment, and revenge, leading to more trauma, endangerment, and revenge.

Thus thinking about aggression as a response to threat makes the vision of the dove also compelling. But the dovish view is often accompanied by a naive sentimentality that seems to suggest that if we were just nicer, more empathic, more thoughtful with one another, aggression and hatred would be generally avoidable. We just need to try harder, the doves tell us, and then we will not fall into the violence that is foreign to our truer natures.

Aggression and Endangerment

The focal point of the controversy around human aggression, on both the philosophical, academic level and the individual, personal level, has been the question of whether aggression is innate or not: is aggression a primary, autonomously arising drive or a response to threat? In recent years, I've come to think that this is not really the most interesting question at all. We get further if we shift our focus away from the aggression itself and onto the ways in which endangerment operates in human affairs.

Let us take as a plausible starting point the dovish view that aggression is a response to threats to survival, either in the immediate present or in the past, either of the individual or of a group (like a country or family) with which the individual strongly identifies. We tend to think of a threat to survival in physical terms—someone standing in front of us wielding a weapon. We might die, so we fight. But human beings, perhaps in contrast to all other animals, form selves, and we tend to experience this sense of self as also having a life and being vulnerable to threat and destruction apart from our physical beings. Under what conditions can I still feel like me? Under what conditions do I feel a dread of psychic annihilation? Under what conditions do I feel an insult to my feelings of worth and value, which undermines my sense of self? Consider the extraordinary phenomenon of road rage, occasionally leading to homicide. The precipitant is almost never a threat of actual bodily harm, but rather a perceived lack of respect. The rageful driver feels "dissed"; the threat is not to survival but to dignity and self-respect. Thus threats to the integrity of the self, subjectively defined, tend to generate powerful aggressive reactions. In fact, the pursuit of revenge provoked by the will to redress past humiliations often propels people into situations that are very dangerous to their actual physical survival.

The problem with the dovish perspective is that relegating aggression to a response to threat seems to imply that aggression is merely incidental and that enhancing our safety would easily eliminate it. But the most interesting and important question is: Why do we seem to be so profoundly and easily threatened?

What distinguishes human beings among our fellow animals is not so much the power or force of our aggression as the prevalence of circumstances in which it is evoked, the ubiquitous conditions in which we feel a threat, not to our physical survival, but to our "self"-preservation. What distinguishes us from our fellow animals is not our capacity for rapacious aggression but our capacity for holding grudges, nursing grievances, imagining insults, and placing ourselves in emotionally vulnerable situations, as in romantic love, that pose threats to our sense of dignity and self-respect.

Child psychologists and psychoanalysts have located the source of our perpetual emotional vulnerability in childhood. Many different forms of endangerment have been described: spiraling physical needs, separation from "attachment" figures, breaks in emotional attunement with caregivers, parental anxiety, maternal impingement breaching the delicate boundaries of the infant self, being interrupted or interfered with, and many more. Under the best of care, infants experience inevitable periods of distress, helplessness, and longing.

One imaginative developmental theory suggests that babies believe that they are suffering because their seemingly omnipotent caregivers must *want* them to suffer. This may seem far-fetched, but the thought that one's pain is intended by another is a recurrent feature not only of infantile but of adult reasoning. Patients in psychoanalysis often feel that their analyst could easily be more helpful if he only cared to. The victim of a stretch of bad luck often feels cursed, imploring the heavens, like Job, and demanding to know "Why me?" For each one of us episodically and for many people chronically, life itself feels cruel, and that very way of framing it personifies an agent whom we consider responsible for our troubles. We feel badly treated, and we are angry in response. And the lover, or the would-be lover, tends to interpret his own sense of hurt and neglect as sure signs of faltering love or uncaring on the part of the beloved.

Desire and Dependency

Consider Jake's bitter hostility toward women. He hated women because of their power over him. In some sense his hatred is under-

standable. It was the hatred of the slave who felt completely exploit-
ed by the master. Jake felt he had betrayed himself, continually
betrayed himself, because he was at the mercy of the women who
aroused his desire and who had total control over his gratification
or frustration. And he wanted revenge. He wanted to turn the
tables. He wanted to restore his own dignity.

But why did Jake experience his desire toward women in terms
of such abject dependency? Was this a perversion of love? Or was
it an exaggeration of an essential dimension of passion?

It was a little of both. Jake's relationships with women were mod-
eled after his relationship with his mother, and that relationship was
striking in its asymmetry: she had been and continued to be very
powerful; he had relied and continued to rely on her for the
resources she distributed, both material and emotional. We might
say that the particular circumstances of Jake's childhood prevented
him from coming to experience himself *as a man* in relation to
women rather than *as a boy* in relation to a mother. He was always
a supplicant longing for and under the control of a person much
more resourceful than he. Alternatively, we might say that the particular circumstances of Jake's childhood made retaining his experience of himself *as a boy,* a favorite son who had good things
bestowed upon him, much more appealing than constructing and
experiencing himself *as a man,* with both resources and vulnerabilities of his own.

For Jake, arousal was experienced as dependency. Sexual desire
had become freighted with nurturance. What was riding on the
woman's response was not just sexual and emotional gratification
but a vision of total care. Of course, such total care is never forth-
coming and can never be. It is as if Jake continually tried to collect
on a promise given to him long ago. The woman who aroused his
desire, the woman who had him in her thrall, was teasing him with

yet more false promises, toying with his longings. And so Jake orchestrated his revenge: by emotionally abandoning the women with whom he had actual relationships, by stalking desirable women and enjoying them without their knowing, outside their control, and by cursing their malevolence and duplicitousness at the very moment he surrendered to them.

The aggression into which romantic passion is prone to collapse is a reflection of the endangered state of the would-be lover. The object of desire has enormous power, and the vulnerability of the lover is proportional to the depth of the love. This stands out in bold relief in the fusion of desire with dependency so prominent in Jake's emotional makeup. Is this a perversion of love? Or is Jake an exaggerated version of Everyman, Everywoman? What is the relationship between desire and dependency? How dangerous does love have to be?

There can be no definitive answer to these questions, because the answers depend on what we *want* love to be. As we have seen, romantic love is not some purely natural phenomenon, like a reflex or nest-building, that has more or less universal, cross-cultural properties. Although it certainly draws upon and uses biological, bodily processes, love is a complex construction, both of a particular historical culture and of the individual lover. The centrality of specific cultural values in the ways we construct love is nowhere more evident than in shifting ideals of love and mental health within psychoanalysis.

In the 1950s the reigning ideology within American psychoanalysis was Freudian ego psychology. The central value in this tradition was a kind of sober, rational, functional maturity. Adaptation and integration were key. The movement from childhood to adulthood entailed a progressive "neutralization" of the irrational, fantastic features of infantile sexual and aggressive wishes and conflicts and the assumption of a steady, consistent, more variegated experience. Intense singular passions, the blacks and whites of childhood were replaced by the grays of adulthood. Perhaps the most important diagnostic distinction during that period was the contrast between "oedipal" and "preoedipal" psychopathology. Oedipal pathology has essentially to do with sexual conflicts originating between ages five and six as infantile sexuality culminates in the child's sexual ambitions toward his parents and his fears of punishment. Preoedipal pathology has essentially to do with earlier, more "primitive" problems of dependency and basic trust in the first several years of life. Jake's fusion of love with dependency suggests preoedipal problems. For the truly oedipal man or woman there is not so much at stake in love, because the earlier dependency issues have been more or less resolved.

As time went on, however, truly oedipal men and women became harder to find. The more psychoanalysts studied and learned about the earliest attachments and relationships between young children and their caregivers, the more issues involving dependency were discovered in everyone's emotional life. I remember worried conversations with classmate/friends during my graduate training in psychology in which we would tentatively admit the horror we felt at discovering *in ourselves* evidence of the preoedipal problems, the conflicts around dependency, we had been reading about in our textbooks. Quite a few analytic theorists today regard the distinction between preoedipal and oedipal, between dependency and desire, as fundamentally porous. Development is now regarded less as a linear sequence of stages, in which a mature version of self replaces an infantile version of self, than as an accretion of new experiences which are additions to rather than replacements for earlier experience.

In the previous chapter we noted the shift in philosophy and psychoanalytic theory in understanding "self" from an earlier view in which healthy individuals possessed *a singular,* integrated self to a more contemporary view of *multiplicitous* selves, emerging in different contexts, for different purposes. This has been accompanied by a closely related shift in thinking about emotions, both in pathology and in health. In the ideal of mental health in the 1950s, emotions were modulated and smoothly fitted together. The pure feelings of childhood were replaced by the ambiguities of adulthood, the loves and hates of immaturity replaced by the healthy integration of complexity and ambivalence in maturity. These days there is considerably more interest in an ideal of mental health in which emotions are experienced vividly and intensely, sometimes in a sequential rather than an integrated fashion. Thus we noted in the previous chapter the enriching importance of the capacity for idealization, alternating with, rather than smoothly integrated into, more pragmatic perspectives.

Similarly, while intense aggression was, in past decades, likely to be regarded as regressive and immature, it is today more often regarded, when interspersed with other intense emotional states, as part of a healthy emotional repertoire, helping to sustain verve and vividness in emotional life. And shared aggressiveness toward others can be an important feature of intimate bonding. There is nothing more dispiriting than getting together with old friends to denigrate common enemies you've hated for years and having someone say, "But wait a minute, they are really not *all* bad."

What has been emerging has been a vision of self-experience in which there is a perpetual shifting resonance among perception and memory, reality and fantasy, present and past, loves and hates. In this way of thinking, intense desire in adult experience, the kind that is stimulated in romantic love, always evokes in some fashion the longings of early childhood. It is the very nature of passion to create a dependence on the object of desire, and the vulnerabilities inherent in adult desire inevitably resonate with one's history of dependence on others. In her haunting short story "The Ballad of the Sad Café" Carson McCullers captured the interpenetrability in romantic love of past with present, childhood with adult longings:

> Love is a joint experience between two persons—but the fact that it is a joint experience does not mean that it is a similar experience to the two people involved. There are the lover and the beloved, but these two come from different countries. Often the beloved is only a stimulus for all the stored-up love which has lain quiet within the lover for a long time hitherto. And somehow every lover knows this. He feels in his soul that his love is a solitary thing. He comes to know a new, strange loneliness and it is this knowledge which makes him suffer.

Jake's problem was not the contamination of desire with dependency, which, as McCullers suggests, is in the very nature of erotic longing. Jake's problem derived from his passive, dependent orientation toward the world, which made the dependency inherent in desire too dangerous to experience in an actual relationship.

Desire, Dependency, and Aggression

In Chapter 2 we considered these questions: Why does sexuality play such a central role in so many people's lives? Why is sexuality so powerful? The received wisdom tells us that the ubiquity and intensity of sexuality derive from its origins as an instinct. If sex is a piece of primitive, raw nature residing in us, it makes sense that it would be universal, powerful, and also aggressive. Nature (in some popular constructions of it) is ruthless. So of course sexuality is also ruthless, a kind of unconscionable pursuit of sheer pleasure with no regard for its object or its consequences.

But what if sexuality is a potential rather than a force? What if the density of the nerve endings in our genitals does not so much push us around from within as offer us the possibility of a unique, exquisite pleasure, greatly enhanced by the participation of another person? One of the most significant features of sexual desire is that it puts us in the position of *needing another*—very much. And perhaps the most significant feature of romantic passion, because of the idealization that steers it, is that we are placing ourselves in the position of *needing a particular other*—very much. It is not just that adult desire in human beings may evoke earlier childhood dependencies (that the oedipal never entirely frees itself from the preoedipal). The power of sexual desire, and the greatly enhanced stakes of romantic passion, are created precisely by the way in which they place us, inevitably so, in a real, not just fantasied, position of dependence upon the desired other.

Consider the pervasiveness of perhaps the most widespread and potent commodity and industry of our time: pornography. In its hard form (X-rated magazines, films, videotapes, and now Internet porn) and in its soft form (R-rated movies, pulp fiction, and the almost constant preoccupation with sexual themes in mainstream magazines, advertising, and television soap operas and situation comedies), pornography delivers sexuality to the adult consumer. How are we to understand this?

We might regard pornography as a response to and consequence of desire, as a measure of the extent of human sexuality out there looking for expression and gratification. But pornography functions not just to gratify sexual desire but also to *generate* arousal. Once past the hormonal surges of adolescence, sexual arousal does not generally simply appear, looking for an outlet, but is rather cultivated. It is stimulated partly from the outside, by the world around us, by other people, by advertising, by the media. (This is why Buddhist meditative retreats are held in the woods.) But sexual arousal is not just provoked by external stimuli; it is also *self*-stimulated. When we reach for a sexually oriented (either explicitly or implicitly) magazine, film, or television show, we are looking to be turned on, aroused. Pornography, in its hard and soft forms, is not just a result of, or a channel for, prior arousal—it plays a very significant role in the self-stimulation of arousal. Rather than being a measure and consequence of the power of naturally occurring sexual desire, pornography is a measure of the extent to which people tend to prefer controlling desire through contrivance rather than being surprised by desire that spontaneously arises.

Do not underestimate the value of contrivance. If I desire you, a real person, and if I long for not just sexual contact but a romantic response, I may be in big trouble. In fact, there is no way to escape big trouble! Because what I want from you makes me dependent upon you, makes me hostage to your feelings toward me, I naturally want to have some control over my fate. What I want is for you to love me, to find me attractive and exciting, precisely when I want you. No matter how much I want to make that happen, I can't, because if I make it happen, it is not what I want. I want you to want me; if I coerce, trick, or manipulate you into wanting me, it doesn't count.

This is what makes the contrivance of pornography so useful. Pornography operates on the "what if?" principle. What if I found myself desiring someone, and what if it happened to be this very person in this picture? on this videotape? on my computer screen? Guess what? I can have him or her. A close cousin of the oldest profession, prostitution, pornography offers the wonderful combination of stimulation in the context of simulation—risk-free desire. It is like shooting fish in a barrel. You can't miss.

The "what-if?" principle works in other ways in the softer forms of pornography and in the celebrity culture that dominates so much of our public life. What if I were him desiring her? or her desiring him? What would that be like? In romantic movies and in soap operas, both on television and in the soap operas the media makes of the lives of celebrities, we go along for the ride at one remove, fully protected. Some people seek the arousal knowingly. They want to dress like their heroes and heroines, have the same handbag, sneakers, couches. There are fans and soap-opera devotees who know they are looking for vicarious romantic thrills. Other people decry all the provocativeness, in fact devote their lives to tracking it down and condemning it. The righteous critics are often seeking the same arousal as the fans, but in a secret form (secret most significantly from themselves).

Why the need for all this control? all this self-protection? It points to just how unprotected and vulnerable we feel when in the throes of uncontrived desire. Dependency is not a holdover from childhood; it is constitutive of desire for a real other person. And the vulnerability of dependency makes us feel endangered. It is not just a fantasy; in desire, we *are* endangered. And being endangered makes us angry. We want to control, to have the power to hurt, perhaps to eliminate the other whose charms have disrupted our equanimity, who has undermined our sense of self and self-worth. Aggression is a response to threat, and sustaining desire over time produces a perpetually regenerated threat.

In *Anna Karenina,* one of the great love stories of all time, Tolstoy informs us that the intense adulterous flirtation between Anna and Vronsky has been sexually consummated in a way that vividly highlights the intense aggression that infuses their desire and presages the violence of Anna's eventual demise:

> That which for nearly a whole year had been the sole desire of
> his life, taking the place of all his former desires; that which for

Anna had been an impossible, dreadful, and for that reason all the more fascinating dream of happiness—that desire had been satisfied. Pale, with trembling lower jaw, he stood over her and implored her to be calm, without knowing himself how and why . . . Looking at him, she felt her degradation physically and she could not utter another word. He felt what a murderer must feel when he looks at the body he has deprived of life. The body he had deprived of life was their love, the first stage of their love. There was something dreadful and loathsome in the recollection of what had been paid for by this terrible price of shame. Shame at her spiritual nakedness crushed her and communicated itself to him. But in spite of the murderer's great horror before the body of his victim, that body has to be cut up and hidden, for the murderer must enjoy the fruits of his crime.

Part of the murderousness of Vronsky's desire for Anna is her marital status as the irreproachable wife of a major public figure; she represents, in her respectability, a challenge to Vronsky's ideology of sexual adventurism and is much more interesting prey than his other dalliances. But the grandeur and power of this novel suggest that Tolstoy is also getting at something far more universal here. *Anna Karenina* is the story of two loves, one tragic, one ending happily. But the love of Levin and Kitty is also hardly a smooth ride. Kitty's ill-fated infatuation with Vronsky nearly destroys her, as her rage toward him is transformed into a murderous self-loathing. And it takes Levin years of withdrawal, sulking, and brooding to recover from Kitty's initial rejection of his protestations of love. Love is a hazardous business, Tolstoy seems to be suggesting. Desire endangers us, and the aggressive response to that endangerment can destroy both the object of desire and ourselves.

In the aftermath of the cataclysms of World War II, popular American culture valued stability above all else, and this was reflected both in the psychoanalytic ideals of integration and adaptation and in popular images of muted marital love. On television, the discreet twin beds were accompanied by an unrelenting civility; we never witnessed a knock-down, drag-out fight between Ozzie and Harriet, or the Andersons (of *Father Knows Best*) or the suggestively named Cleavers (of *Leave It to Beaver*).

Contemporary ideals, both popular and psychoanalytic, have come to put more emphasis on vitality, creativity, and authenticity and less on safety and stability. This has laid the groundwork for the reconstruction of romance as a viable adult experience, something more than an adolescent regression. But constructing romantic passion in a way that allows for its risks and its fragility requires coming to terms with the dependency and aggression that are its necessary companions. This makes long-term relationships built upon the ideal of safety and collusive, illusory predictability an infertile ground for passion, which needs space for aggression to breathe.

Strategies of Control

Some theorists of the erotic have suggested that aggression and sadism play major roles in sexual desire because we long to redress the humiliations we all have suffered as children in connection with our early longings. Intense desire, in this view, is always fused with a thirst for revenge. Like Vronsky, each one of us wants to bring down our Anna, to murder her power to arouse our longings. Passionate desire, in this view, is much more likely to arise in new relationships with alluring but unknown strangers. The very caring that may develop in long-term relationships, it is argued, inhibits aggression, making the erotic features of romance impossible. But I believe it is actually the other way around—that long-standing love is rife with aggression. The problem is not in its absence but in the intense danger of its presence.

Are anonymous relationships with strangers more fertile ground for generating the kinds of aggression that add an edge to desire? I think not. The momentary aggressive fantasies I generate in relation to strangers are nothing compared with the intensity of the homicidal fantasies I harbor toward those I live with and love most deeply. And the effectiveness and danger of aggression are directly proportional to how much one knows about its target. I have had several patients with blocks in their connection with and capacity to express aggression who have made strides in overcoming their inhibitions in this regard by yelling at taxi drivers (usually for good reasons). They were certainly not lacking anger and hatred in their intimate relationships. But the time-limited duration of the taxi rides and the option of jumping out at the next traffic light made that venue a safer one for experimenting with dreaded feelings. If aggression is a key ingredient of passion, there is plenty of it to be found in long-standing relationships.

It is the very otherness of the other that defines the limits to one's own omnipotence and creates the vulnerability, often the experience of helplessness, that accompanies desire. Thus romantic longing skates always on the edge of humiliation. This is why objects of desire are so easily transformed into objects of revenge. It is their fault that one desires them, as if their very desirability were an instrument of torture.

Aggression is the underbelly of desire, and this is one reason romance is so fragile. Sustaining romance requires tolerating a sense of vulnerability and aggression. The deeper the passion, the more precarious the vulnerability and the more potentially destructive the aggression. The capacity to contain aggression thus is a precondition for the capacity to love, and sustaining romantic passion requires a delicate balancing act.

There are many different strategies for managing the confluence of love and hate in romance. The basic underlying principle is to

both express and control the aggression at the same time by dimin-
ishing or obliterating the object of desire. Aesop long ago identified
this common solution as "sour grapes": the seemingly desirable
other that disappoints was rotten all along. There might be good
grapes out there somewhere, but self-protection against disappointment requires constant reminders not to expect any sweetness
from one's own bunch. Denigration thus serves the purpose of
maintaining equilibrium, and a chronic contempt for one's long-
term partner often feels like a necessary requirement for stability.

In some cases, excitement and longing are preserved as memories. There is a nostalgic sense of an earlier time, at the beginning of
the relationship, when it was safe to love. But that innocence is gone
now; it was betrayed. The other has demonstrated how false were
those promises of love. As with Cathy and Carl, whom we met in
Chapter 3, excitement hovers always as a potential danger. It feels
crucial to preserve a kind of vigilance against memories of early
excitement, to feed hurts and resentments as a necessary constant
reminder of the dangers of desire.

Human emotional life is intense, varied, and conflictual. One of
the most popular unconscious strategies for coping with this density
is the segregation of different feelings among intimates, as, for
example, the members of a family. Often one member of the family
becomes the "sensitive" one, another the tough one, another the
explosive one, and so on. Each, of course, has the whole range of
emotions, but each counts on the others to bear and represent the
emotions that he or she has trouble containing within his or her own
conscious experience.

In couples, security is often maintained and aggression regulated
through such segregation and reversals, often along lines made easy
by traditional gender roles. It is not that I want her and therefore
feel dependent upon her, declares the pseudo-self-sufficient man,

but that she wants and desperately needs me. I could easily live without her; there is a world of difference between her abject need of me and my toughness and self-sufficiency. I stay with her only out of pity. These situations maintain a stability as long as the other plays her part as the needful, dependent pursuer. It is striking how frequently the disdainful, self-sufficient object of pursuit panics and suddenly becomes desperately needful when his pursuer finally gives up. It then becomes clear that the triad of desire, dependency, and aggression that constitutes romantic passion had been split and segregated, one partner feeling and displaying only desire and dependency, the other partner feeling and displaying only aggressive contempt.

Sexual dysfunction often plays a key role in risk management by couples over time. It seems crucial not to get too excited about the other, and diminished excitement serves the purposes at once of self-protection and revenge. I was once excited about you, the diminished arousal seems to be expressing, but there is not much to get excited about now. Often lovers work together to pretend they are safer (even if also a bit sadder) over time, by collapsing their expectations of each other in collusively arranged, choreographed routine. Each feels the other is less exciting because of being so familiar and predictable. And each acts toward the other in as wholly and artificially predictable a fashion as possible. But, of course, lowering expectations also empties out passion. No risk, no gain.

Passionate hatred derives from humiliation and endangerment to the self. Because romance generates hope, longing, and dependency, and because hope, longing, and dependency always risk humiliation, love is necessarily dangerous. Aggression is love's shadow, an inextricable accompaniment and necessary constituent of romantic passion. The degradation of romance is not due to the contamination of love by aggression but to the inability to sustain the necessary tension between them. Since the effectiveness of aggression is directly proportional to how much one knows about one's target, aggression is much more dangerous in long-standing love relationships than with strangers; the capacity to love over time entails the capacity to tolerate and repair hatred.

5

Guilt and Self-Pity

We are on the run. We believe happiness is a matter
of geography, or a matter of class, or of color, or that
happiness hides its wiles inside a pile of money.
Motion to *somewhere* is what we wish for. All along
the run, the blues disturbs and reminds us, hiding like
a pebble inside our favorite jogging shoes or sitting
just under our skin, a long splinter of emotional
recognition denied. The blues never refuses to tell us
whenever we are fugitives from the mirror.

—STANLEY CROUCH

WE ARE OUR STORIES, our accounts of what has happened to
us. It is not our memories alone that sustain a sense of personhood.
The past is too multifaceted and full of details. To have a self, we
need a protagonist, someone who does things and to whom things
happen. The past needs to be organized into a narrative, or several
alternative narratives. No stories, no self.

The stories of a life can be told in many different ways, for many
different purposes. Sometimes one tells one's story to elicit particular feelings in the listener: admiration, excitement, arousal, understanding, or pity. Sometimes one tells one's story to stir the listener
to action, to stimulate: help, opposition, collaboration, or submis-

sion. And, of course, each of us has many stories to tell. Lifetimes are full of different kinds of experiences.

For most of us, our romantic fate, the account of our romantic life, is a central, recurrent narrative within the stories we tell others about ourselves and the stories we tell ourselves about ourselves to maintain a sense of who we are. And no romantic narrative, if it is to avoid degenerating into a fairy tale (and they lived happily ever after), is without pain, hurt, and loss. That is why the blues is such a popular musical genre.

In romance, as in life in general, there is perhaps no better way to determine one's identity, to symbolize one's uniqueness, than to catalogue the scars that serve as the remains and reminders of past injuries. Homer understood this. Part of what keeps Homer's *Odyssey* fresh and relevant to contemporary readers is its rich reflections on the theme of identity, the question of what makes a person the *particular* person he is. Who is Odysseus, the hero of Troy, in each new adventure, with its different set of circumstances and its different cast of characters?

There are situations, as with the Cyclops, in which Odysseus's concealment of his identity saves him. "I am nobody," he tells the Cyclops. After being blinded by Odysseus, the Cyclops screams in his agony, "Nobody has blinded me," thereby ensuring the futility of his calls for help. In other situations, as on the island of Circe, Odysseus saves himself by securing Athena's help to preserve his identity, preventing Circe from turning him into a barnyard animal as she has done to his crew. Then again, when he does reach Ithaca, everything depends upon Odysseus's concealment of his identity, so he can prepare for his revenge against the suitors of his wife, Penelope. Master of disguises, he transforms himself into a beggar. Yet he is recognized by the old servant who had been his nurse years before. How? Penelope asks her to bathe the old beggar, and the servant recognizes a scar on his leg, the result of an encounter with a wild boar during a hunting accident in his youth. When all is said and done, Homer tells us, we are recognizable, both to others and to ourselves, by our scars, by old wounds, by damage inflicted by life.

The psychoanalytic process may be characterized as the exposure and consideration of such scars, old wounds, damaging encounters with life. "See what has happened to me," the analysand tells the analyst, sometimes in narrative form, sometimes through unintentional, indirect revelation (as with Odysseus's scar), and sometimes through reenactments in which the analysand and the analyst unknowingly play out old, painful scenarios. As the scars and wounds of past and present injuries are displayed, the question "Why?" is never far off. Why did this happen? The analysand needs to determine this to make sense of the past, to account for the present, and to guide himself in the future. And answers to "Why?" tend to gravitate toward two contrasting poles: "This damage was inflicted upon me through no fault of my own," or "I brought this upon myself and others." Consequently, life stories are sorted out around the axis of self-pity and guilt.

In narratives of romance, accounts of one's fate in love, self-pity takes the form of victimization: "She done me wrong" is the central theme. Self-pity organizes stories of relationships both past and present: loves in which one has been betrayed or abandoned, and present relationships in which one lives with a perpetual sense of disappointment and renunciation. In other narratives of romance, guilt suggests a betrayal not by the other but by oneself: "I was a fool" is the central theme. Guilt often organizes stories of past relationships: one's faithlessness or lack of devotion drove one's true love away. And guilt often organizes stories of present relationships: one lives with a perpetual sense of being undeserving, unworthy of a love that is at hand but cannot be enjoyed.

A brief episode with one of my analysands highlighted for me both the surprising ways in which personal stories are brought to life in psychoanalysis and the centrality of the self-pity/guilt axis in making sense of those stories.

Bearing Responsibility

Ed was an engaging, talented man in his forties who had grown up as the only child of immigrant parents. Survivors of the Holocaust, his parents had lost most of their family members. They suffered from chronic depression and guilt. They regarded Ed as the embodiment both of all their hopes in the "new world" and of their subsequent disappointment that their profound pain and losses could never be made whole again. Ed had experienced intense struggles for independence from his parents in his adolescence and young adulthood and had built a rich and fulfilling life for himself. Yet he suffered from bouts of depression and explosive rage. And his close relationships were strangled by tentacles of guilt, the residue of his childhood. He had long feared psychoanalysis as another entanglement, but recent successes in several areas of his life had emboldened him to face his childhood demons and begin analytic treatment. We had accomplished considerable important work over the course of about a year when the following situation arose.

Ed was my first patient on one morning of the week. He needed to schedule some urgent dental work into his busy life and asked me if I could meet with him half an hour early so as to make the dental appointment possible. I am an early riser, so this did not pose much of a sacrifice. I agreed to the arrangement for the following week.

On the appointed day, a clear but cold winter morning, I bought some coffee, as is my custom, on a corner near my office and was somewhat absentmindedly making my way along, fighting the icy wind coming off the Hudson River. As soon as I saw Ed in front of my building, I realized I had forgotten our agreement. I had thought I was five minutes early; actually I was twenty-five minutes late. He greeted me by saying, "So, *you're* a creature of habit." "I'm really sorry," I said, "I just completely forgot."

Ed was silent as he settled onto the couch. I asked myself whether my forgetting about the change in time had something to do with my feelings about Ed and our relationship that we would need to address. There was some inconvenience in the rescheduling, but that was minor. I decided the real problem was my failure to write the change into my appointment book. Up until a few years ago, I hardly ever wrote anything down in my appointment book and was able to remember what I needed to do. With the encroachment of age, my memory had become less reliable. I was increasingly forgetting things like this, but my narcissism seemed to prevent me from using my book, memory crutch that I considered it to be. All of this seemed not terribly relevant to Ed and his experience, so I suspended my reflections on my forgetting. Ed sometimes, quite usefully, took some time at the beginning of sessions to assess his emotional state. On this day I was mindful of how little time we had. I felt it was important to talk about what had happened, since I would not be seeing him for several days, including a weekend. So I started by saying, "That must have been really difficult for you."

At first, Ed reported, when he began to realize that I must have forgotten, he had felt "great." We had often spoken of his need to regard me as an ideal figure in every respect, under whose tutelage he would also become perfect. And he was indeed a very conscientious analysand. Recently he'd been going through rough times, and had not felt very good about himself at all. So for about the first ten or fifteen minutes of the session he was forced to experience outdoors on his own, he felt an enormous sense of relief. I had screwed

up. If I was not perfect, he too could be imperfect without having
to feel so bad about himself.

However, it was cold outside my building. "As I began to freeze
my ass off," he recounted, "I began to get angry." "It was great that
I screwed up," I suggested, "but it would have been better if I had
screwed up not quite so much." He lingered upon both his relief
and his anger for a while, and then shifted the focus to what I had
come to recognize as his characteristic self-recriminations. How
petty of him to feel relief at my failings, he pointed out. Why did he
need to maintain this self-destructive idealization of me in the first
place?

I began to have the sense, at once both reassuring and disquiet-
ing, that I was being let gently off the hook. I found myself saying
something like this: "Your relief and also your anger about my forgetting are really important. It seems to me that they bring us into
a different sort of relationship with each other. By falling back into
your self-recriminations about idealizing me in the first place, I feel
you are letting me off the hook and tucking us both back into more
familiar and more comfortable roles." As I said this, I was struck by
the oddness of my choice of the word "tucking." I then had an association to a story Ed had told me about his childhood.

As a boy Ed had spent a great deal of time day-dreaming, and also
sometimes night-dreaming, about World War II. There were recurrent scenes of his parents and other relatives being trapped in per-
ilous situations, with Ed managing heroic rescues, saving them and
himself as well. He had fallen into playing a game when he went to
sleep at night in which he would enclose himself under his sheets
and blankets, sealing himself off. He would quietly smother himself
until, at the last desperate moment, he would throw off the covers,
gasping for air. I found this story poignant, and recognized its connection to my description of Ed's "tucking" us both back into our

customary roles, me as presumably ideal and him as flawed, guilty, and conscientious.

Ed responded to my suggestion about his letting me off the hook, and I shared my association to his suffocation game. He noted how difficult it was for him to find ways of regarding either himself or me as other than a heroic ideal or an utter failure. We spoke about how caring in his family was defined in terms of desperation and upset, goodness in terms of sacrifice and heightened intensity. I suggested that in their passionate involvement in the son they needed him to be, his parents had rarely gotten to know the boy and then the man he was. I floated the possibility that my forgetting might have been a way for me to escape the suffocating role of perfection I was assigned. He described the world of options between heroic ideals and utter failures as a "no-man's-land" in which he had trouble staying for very long. Then Ed had to leave to keep his dentist appointment, and the shortened session came to an end.

Several sessions later, Ed began by talking about his anger over the bill I had given him. I hadn't quite known what to do about the abbreviated session, which had been slightly longer than one-third our usual time. So I had charged him one-third of our usual fee, and Ed was very angry about my decision. He felt that given my forgetting, and given his "freezing his ass off" outside my building, I should have not charged him at all. It seemed petty, strikingly ungenerous. It seemed to reflect a failure to take responsibility for my own mistake. Did I think it didn't matter that I had kept him waiting? He had come to think of me as responsible and caring, gracious and generous, along with various other ideal qualities. This was annoying and really disappointing.

We spent considerable time exploring Ed's reactions, during which I was silently scurrying around in my own mind trying to figure out what I thought about his blistering attack. At first I felt like a creep. I certainly had felt bad about my uncharacteristic lateness. Why hadn't I just waived the fee for the third of a session? It certainly *seemed* petty. I remembered briefly considering and then rejecting the idea of not charging him, without fully spelling out my own reasons to myself. I felt I owed him an explanation. So I began to explain why I had decided to include a partial session on the bill. I wasn't completely sure what I was going to say as I began to speak, but I felt confident that wherever this went it would be relevant and important.

I said that I hadn't felt at all flippant about my lateness—that I had felt bad about it. Yet I hadn't seriously considered not charging him, and I wasn't sure why not. The money itself was not important and seemed an insignificant amount to both of us. It would have been easy enough to forget about it. But it seemed to me that I would have been appeasing him, buying him off, if I hadn't charged him. I was curious about his feeling that the appropriate way to deal with guilt is to make a reparative gesture of some sort.

This led to a comparison between our approaches to guilt. For Ed, guilt required compensation, even if only symbolic—some form of apology and reparation to set things right and to set the stage for forgiveness. Failure to make the gesture suggests an avoidance of responsibility and an absence of genuine regret. For me, one of the main features of guilt is that it is difficult to bear. One way not to bear it is to do penance or enact rituals to erase it. We teach our children to say magic words like "please," "thank-you," and "I'm sorry." I've finally come to believe that magic words and gestures don't count for much in themselves. When I feel wronged, I much prefer that the other persons spend time thinking about *why* they did what they did so they won't do it again rather than offer penitent gestures. I felt that not charging Ed would have been irresponsible because it would have enabled me fairly easily to shift from feeling bad to feeling magnanimous.

As with most useful events in psychoanalysis, exploring the rippling associations to our interaction proved more important than any decision arrived at. In many respects, the issues involved in our early morning episode represented a microcosm of Ed's struggle with his parents, as well as the central motifs in all his romantic involvements with women.

What precisely is the relationship between pain and guilt? Between his parents' demands for reparations for Ed's boyhood failures and the formal reparations of the postwar German government? How does one evade guilt? How does one best bear guilt? A striking aspect of the issue before us was the close relationship between Ed's pain and victimization and my guilt. He could have left after it was clear that I had forgotten the session. In some respects, his very conscientiousness and the pain it cost him, his very suffering, laced with a subtle self-pity, partially caused and determined the amount of my guilt.

Several months later Ed's mother blamed him for causing her pain by not asking her about the results of a doctor's appointment that he had not even known about. This became the occasion for returning to the topic of his vigil outside my door that cold morning. As we spelled out the details of his system of emotional double-entry bookkeeping, it became clearer why he felt it was important to build up "credits" in relation to me. I had done something to make him suffer. And the more he suffered at my hands, the more protection he had against future attacks in which *I* would assign *him* guilt for causing *me* pain. This double-entry bookkeeping, we later discovered, was a key reason Ed's romantic relationships with women tended to drift into a measured distance. Passion and desire receded into the background as hurts and the resulting credits were carefully noted and collected.

The Zero-Sum Game

Guilt and self-pity often have a complex relationship. Sometimes they are locked together in a kind of zero-sum game: the more there is of one, the less there is of the other. Couples frequently collude in creating this kind of complementarity in their most hateful fights. In the intricate reciprocity required for passionate intensity, each is both the victim of the other's insensitivity and cruelty and the intentional and unintentional agent of the other's pain. In prototypical couple arguments, both participants highlight their own victimization and minimize their own agency, elaborating self-pity and dodging guilt. The zero-sum premise locks such arguments in futility. Each feels his or her pain is real. And both conclude that to feel guilty, to assume some responsibility for the pain of the other amounts to surrendering claims for pity and responsibility in the other. The couple's ability to gradually work their way free of the zero-sum assumption can unlock such arguments. Each member of the couple can tentatively acknowledge that both have been both objects and agents, or, in Albert Camus's terms, both victims and executioners. The pain of each is real and requires acknowledgment; the failure of each is real and requires accountability.

Self-pity and guilt can also become locked in a zero-sum game within the mind of a single individual. Children who grow up in abusive or chaotic households exist in a reality that is too frightening and painful to accept. Because it is impossible to live in a world in which they are the victims of so much random abuse, so much undeserved suffering, they organize their narratives about their own experience around the presumption of their own guilt. To truly pity themselves, to directly face the hopeless impossibility of their situation, is simply unbearable. It must be their own badness that causes their caregivers to abuse them; if they were good, this nightmare would not be happening.

On a microcosmic level this strategy plays out the problem that has daunted theists since the advent of religious belief systems anchored in the conviction that God is both all-powerful and just. The suffering of humankind, especially that of innocent children, has been difficult to reconcile with an omnipotent and fair deity. The most compelling answer in many religious traditions has been the assumption of human guilt. From pagan notions of insulted and offended gods to the subtleties of the doctrine of original sin, humankind has tended to purchase culpability in exchange for relief from a sense of pitiful helplessness. As the Scottish psychoanalyst W. R. D. Fairbairn put it, "it is better to be a sinner in a world ruled by God than to live in a world ruled by the Devil."

Thus a contrived sense of guiltiness can serve as a psychological defense against a more genuine sense of pathos or sadness for oneself. And conversely, a contrived sense of self-pity sometimes serves as a psychological defense against a more genuine sense of guilt. These are situations in which elaborating one's victimization at the hands of others operates as a preemptive defense against taking responsibility for one's own failings.

Pathos and guilt are fundamental features of romantic narratives. In the previous chapter we explored dependency and aggression as inevitable accompaniments of desire. Dependency thwarted leads to pathos, and given the lifetime of longings we bring to romantic love, dependency is always, to some extent, thwarted, even in the most satisfying of romantic relationships. The proximity of aggression to love leads to guilt, and given the intense vulnerability generated by romantic love, aggression (and therefore guilt) is always close by.

Both self-pity and guilt come in many forms, and distinguishing among these forms is tricky. The psychoanalytic literature has provided little illumination about self-pity, but psychoanalytic authors have had a lot to say about guilt. The basic approach was set by

Freud and then revolutionized by Melanie Klein. So in trolling the world of psychoanalytic ideas for ways of thinking about the place of guilt in the experience of romance, we will begin with their understanding of the origins and nature of guilt.

Psychoanalytic Accounts of Guilt

Guilt was central to Freud's understanding of human difficulties, both neurotic and universal. In Freud's vision, our psychological lives are bi-phasic. Before and beneath the life we know and remember is another, earlier life of childhood sexuality, now shrouded in infantile amnesia. That life was both wondrous and terrifying, body-centered and full of polymorphously perverse sexuality and phantasmagoric aggression. For each small child that earlier life culminates in reenacting the role of Sophocles' Oedipus. Our sexual ambitions lead us to alternately both desire our parents and plot their murder. Each of us becomes implicated in the most psychologically horrifying of crimes—incest and parricide. And each of us becomes a social, responsible being through fear of punishment and retaliation and the assumption of guilt for those forbidden impulses: the external objects of our desire and hatred are replaced by internal objects of conscience and surveillance, and the darkness of repression falls across our earlier life.

For Freud, guilt is the linchpin of our ascent from the bestial to the civilized. An absence of oedipal guilt results in sociopathy, the most socially dangerous form of character pathology. An abundance of oedipal guilt results in neurosis, in which the sufferer unconsciously arranges elaborate symptoms that provide both expression of and punishment for infantile sexual wishes. An overabundance of oedipal guilt results in the sorry state Freud called the "negative therapeutic reaction." The neurotic comes to psychoanalysis for relief but cannot allow himself to benefit from it. As the oedipal criminal he unconsciously takes himself to be, he regards himself as undeserving of help: his crimes are unpardonable.

The Viennese-born English analyst Melanie Klein, who has had an enormous impact on psychoanalytic ideas since the 1930s, added a powerful new dimension to Freud's account of guilt. For Klein, guilt appears not, as Freud thought, at age five or six, in the culmination of the oedipal stage, but much earlier, in the infant's *pre*-oedipal relationship to the breast. Klein's vision of the infant's mental state is darker and more troubled than Freud's, dominated by intense, rageful murderousness and psychotic anxieties. But the infant also loves the breast and its transformative milk. Thus Klein's infant is rent between abject longings and profound, loving gratitude for the transcendent goodness of the available, satisfying breast, and rageful, hateful destructiveness toward the merciless malevolence of the unavailable, unsatisfying breast. Because these two experiences are so discordant, the infant's early weeks are spent in a psychological organization Klein termed the "paranoid-schizoid position," in which there are, in fact, two breasts—one good and one bad, a breast that is the object of one's love and a breast that is the object of one's hatred.

Gradually, Klein believed, the two breasts, and the two divergent experiences of mothering they represent, become one. In this enormously difficult and unstable psychological achievement, which Klein termed the "depressive position," the infant loves and hates the very same object. When this ("whole") object is satisfying, its good milk suffuses the infant with love and safety, inside and out, and the deepest love and gratitude are evoked in the child. When this ("whole") object is unsatisfying, when the infant is left at the mercy of his own hunger, or fed milk that feels digestively disruptive rather than soothing, the infant is overtaken by the most global and unforgiving of rages. In his fantasy, which is the only reality he knows, he destroys the ("whole") object that has failed him, and suddenly finds himself bereft. In his uncontrollable, vengeful retaliation, he has destroyed the very source of love and goodness in his world. He has orphaned himself and rendered his world desolate.

One of Klein's greatest achievements was her account of the emergence, in the midst of this self-generated, apocalyptic devastation, of what she called an urge for "reparation." The infant realizes that the object he has hatefully destroyed is also the object he deeply loves; he is gripped by profound regret and guilt. In his fantasy, which is the only reality he knows, he desperately repairs the ("whole") object that he hates but also loves, the both satisfying and frustrating object that he must episodically destroy and rebuild. In Klein's vision, the shifting balance between the child's guilt-driven, loving reparation and his hateful destructiveness is the key factor that determines the child's and later the adult's emotional life. If the hate is too strong and the trust in one's reparative capacities too weak, relatedness to whole objects cannot be sustained, and there is a retreat back into the split world of the paranoid-schizoid position. Now there are two objects once again, all good and all bad, with love and hate safely segregated from each other. But in the paranoid-schizoid world, which in today's diagnostic lingo is called the world of the "borderline" patient, the fuller humanity both of the self and of the other cannot be contained. For Freud, oedipal guilt is the gateway from later childhood into human civilization; for Klein, preoedipal guilt of infancy is the central developmental achievement that makes human love possible.

These traditional psychoanalytic accounts of guilt have narrative power and clinical richness. They also have two features in common, which have had an important bearing on the ways analytic clinicians have applied them in therapeutic strategies. In both

accounts, the crimes for which the guilt-ridden parties hold themselves accountable took place in the distant past of early childhood;
and, equally important, the crimes never actually occurred.

Consequently, the way guilt is managed in most traditional psychoanalytic accounts goes something like this: Patients come to
realize that they are at odds with themselves in fundamental
respects, that they sabotage their own ambitions, either through
symptoms or through maladaptive character traits. Such self-
sabotage derives from guilt, and the guilt is traceable to various
imagined crimes of infancy and childhood. Patients come to realize
that, in the fantasy-driven mind of a child, they treated wishes as
equivalent to acts. They wanted to commit incest and parricide, but
did not. Yet they punish themselves as if they had. They wanted to
destroy the frustrating breast, but did not. Yet they punish themselves as if they had. So patients in analysis come to forgive themselves their imagined transgressions, to hold themselves less
accountable. As the adults they have become, they pardon the child
they were for crimes they never committed.

The American psychoanalyst Hans Loewald introduced a different spin on this standard approach. Loewald suggested that it was
a mistake to view childhood guilt as deriving only from fantasies in
the child's mind. Viewing the Oedipus complex in terms of genera-
tional struggle, Loewald argued that the child necessarily kills something in the parents, not just in fantasy but in actuality. The small
child requires total care, and an important and precious version of
the parent comes alive through the provision of that loving nurturance. But the growing child needs to renounce that care, to kill that
version of the parent. No matter how happy parents are to see their
children grow, they cannot easily renounce the pleasures and
responsibilities that earlier developmental stages entailed. Parents
always exit conflictedly, never simply gracefully, from each devel-

opmental stage. And the child, who needs to struggle toward his own emancipatory freedom, must do his part in pushing the parent off. That murder brings guilt, and bearing that guilt is an important part of psychological growth.

Similarly the vulnerability and dependency generated by the romantic longings of adulthood produce genuine, adult aggression toward the object of desire. Love is risky not only in early childhood but at all points in life, and guilt is prompted by the aggression that inevitably accompanies love in adulthood. Not all guilt can usefully be reduced to the real or imagined crimes, oedipal or preoedipal, of childhood. I learned a great deal about this from another patient, Will, who, it quickly became clear, sought analytic treatment because of a deep, unrelenting sense of guilt.

Guilt as a Refuge from Guilt

Will suffered from bad dreams. In his mid-forties, he worked as a high-level corporate executive with considerable responsibilities. He worried about making mistakes. He worried about forgetting something important. He worried about hurting people through oversight or by making the wrong decisions. He had nightmares in which he was enmeshed in business problems and discovered he had overlooked something crucial, leading to disastrous consequences. The dreams seriously disrupted his sleep, and he arrived for the first session looking as if he hadn't slept for months.

Will was raised in the South in a fundamentalist Christian subculture. Although no longer actively religious, he had retained a deep commitment to some of the values by which he had been raised. He was very principled in many ways I found admirable. He was also distrustful of psychoanalysis and the culture of popular psychology. Although his wife and many of his New York City friends had been in one sort of therapy or another, Will tended to regard therapy as self-indulgent. He considered most talk about the unconscious a form of self-deception and bad faith. But he could not comprehend the worries and nightmares from which he was suffering and warily decided to give therapy a try.

In exploring the phenomenology of these bad dreams and the sense of the world they portrayed, Will began to talk about the first and most dramatic circumstances in which he had found himself worrying about not attending to something important, events he regarded as the most fateful and formative in his adult life.

Following what he remembered as a very happy childhood and a relatively smooth and successful early adulthood, in his mid twenties Will was married to Gail, whom he loved. Gail was pregnant and would soon give birth to a son. However, several months earlier Will had begun what seemed an innocent flirtation with Linda, a woman in his office. It had slowly developed into an affair. Initially he had had no intention of acting on their mutual attraction, but little by little he got more involved. There was something extraordinarily powerful for him about being with Linda. He was amazed that he could actually carry off the affair in a fashion that seemed to have no impact at all on his marriage. Finally, Will realized he was deeply, passionately, dangerously involved, and he tried to break it off, recommitting himself to his marriage. But he couldn't stop thinking about Linda, and each time he resolved to stop seeing her, he was unable to follow through. During his trysts with Linda, he was increasingly worried that something terrible might happen to his wife and, especially his son, while he was out of touch. This was the origin of the feeling he recognized in the dreams that now tormented him.

Will had begun to realize he did not know himself, and that made him suffer greatly. After a final, futile effort to renounce Linda, he decided to leave his wife. This felt agonizingly difficult because he regarded it as a criminal act, but he felt unable to stay in the marriage. He lived for several years in a self-imposed purgatory of solitude, unable to allow himself to be with either woman. Finally Linda presented him with an ultimatum—marry her or their relationship was over. Only because of that externally imposed threat was Will able to create a new life with Linda. They married and had two daughters; he remained a caring and responsible father to his first child. What is more, his second marriage was much more passionate and engaged him more fully and deeply than his first. Yet he was racked by guilt.

Will never stopped feeling that what he had done to Gail and his son was unforgivable. He had betrayed his marriage vows, which he had made in absolute good faith. He had hurt his wife profoundly and made his son's early years complicated and difficult. And he had done all this purely out of his own selfish motives—his lust. His account of his own life assumed a biblical tone: he had fallen from grace, and his sin was a mortal one. The more deeply we explored his life, the clearer it became that his fall, more than twenty years before, was the central organizing event. Even though he loved Linda and his daughters, he secretly felt his second marriage was not real. It was the consequence of a crime, a lie, like a house built on sand. In dealing with his ex-wife, he never stopped seeing her as a victim. Even though Gail had remarried and built a successful life for herself, even though their son appeared happy and was doing remarkably well as far as anyone could tell, Will regarded his abandonment of his first family as having inflicted a wound from which there was no recovery, from which the victims were still hemorrhaging.

In the legal settlement of their marriage, Will had therefore given Gail more than she had asked for; in their negotiations over time about their son, Will was constantly yielding to Gail's convenience.

Gail was an only child, whereas Will had many siblings. Will felt that his son should be with his mother and her parents on all major holidays, since his absence would be so painful for them. Consequently, his son spent little time with Will's extended family, a rich and colorful brood of uncles, aunts, and cousins.

As we explored his subtle assumptions about these situations, it became apparent that Will was convinced that he had no rights at all. At any moment, Gail could, and sometimes did, bring up his abandonment of them. At any time he could again be branded as guilty. Perhaps if Will was extraordinarily nice and generous, perhaps if he was more than conscientious, perhaps if he suffered on and on, perhaps someday Gail would forgive him. But of course she never did. And, in negotiations about where his son would be on various holidays, he continued to picture Gail's family's dinner as the scene from Dickens's *A Christmas Carol* after Tiny Tim's death. Seated around the table were Carol and her parents—and then there was the empty chair, the son's chair, the one whose emptiness Will would be responsible for if he insisted on spending time with his son. As in another Dickens tale, it was as though Miss Havisham's clock had stopped; time was frozen at the moment of his crime.

Will hated what he regarded as the facile psychologizing of contemporary culture. He hated political figures who had done horrible things, both to their constituents and to people close to them, who sought public forgiveness by disclosing their indiscretions, congratulated themselves on their honesty, and asked for the voters' continued support in the next election. He believed psychology often provided people with an easy and dishonest way out: "I was traumatized as a kid—abused and abandoned. I was wronged, or confused. My unconscious made me do it." Will thought psychoanalysis dangerous, and that certainly included our work together, because he did not want to let himself off the hook in the easy way he imagined it provided. He firmly believed he was guilty of something terrible, and he did not want to purchase a self-deceiving absolution for his crime.

I agreed with much of what Will said about the irresponsibility and facile self-exoneration typical of contemporary public life. I admired his honesty and the high standards to which he held himself. But I began to feel he had suffered enough. There was something self-indulgent in his self-mortification. Will regarded my views about his guilt as dangerous. They lured him into a self-forgiveness he experienced as a self-betrayal. Over a period of months we discussed many different facets of his life, but we kept returning to the problem of his guilt, his densely packed self-accusations, on which he, and then he and I, appeared to be deadlocked.

An opening occurred when I realized (and found a way to make him curious about) how punishing his guilt was. It punished not just himself, who, he believed, deserved all punishments, but those around him as well. I wondered how his son would feel after he grew up and realized that he had been deprived of becoming part of his father's extended family. This potential source of richness for his son was being sacrificed to Will's efforts to appease Gail. And then there was Linda. In some deep sense, Will could never fully give himself to her as a legitimate husband. There were also his two daughters, whom he cared about a great deal but had difficulty in fathering without conflict. We began to realize that his inability to come to terms with his earlier "crime" involved him in continually destructive patterns with those he loved. It was as if his self-mortification erected an altar upon which his current relationships were sacrificed.

There was a magical, almost delusional dimension to Will's guilt. Even though circumstances had changed, Will refused to. He continued longing for a forgiveness that would undo the damage. He was unable to accept the loss of an ideal image of himself, the image he had shattered. He wanted to be made whole again. What struck us both with great surprise was the realization that Will, who seemed to be the guiltiest man alive, had actually arranged his life around a refusal to truly bear his guilt. His appeasement and self-punishment were all aimed at erasing the consequences of his actions, which he was simply unwilling to accept. Thus self-inflicted or arranged punishment, while appearing to acknowledge culpability, often operates as a diversion from experiencing guilt that feels too difficult to bear.

Pathos and Self-Pity

Guilt and self-pity appear deceptively simple because they are feelings. We tend to regard feelings as just existing—pure, unbidden, and uncomplicated bursts of emotion. But feelings of guilt and self-pity really originate in complex attitudes we take toward ourselves. With both guilt and self-pity, there occurs a split in the self: a part or version of the self assumes an attitude, accusatory in guilt and compassionate in self-pity, toward another part or version of the self. The source from which feelings of guilt and self-pity emerge is a particular kind of multifaceted relationship we have with ourselves, in which we are both subject and object. Psychoanalysts have labeled these relationships "internal object relations" and regard them as the deep structure of all our experience. This underlying relational structure makes feelings of guilt and self-pity quite complex.

Of all the human emotions, we are perhaps most ambivalent about pity. Pathos in music, art, religious iconography, and literature functions as a powerful, highly valued quality that enhances our humanity. A strong capacity for pity toward one's fellow human beings is associated with compassion and considered a virtue. Aristotle defines pity as "pain at . . . an appearing evil, destructive or painful, belonging to one who does not deserve to have it happen— the sort of evil that one might expect oneself to suffer, or some member of one's family." In her discussion of Aristotle's concept of pity, Martha C. Nussbaum stresses that he regards the object of pity as undeserving of the evil befalling him, and this explains the complementary relationship between pity and guilt: "The (believed) goodness of the individual object of pity . . . reinforces the belief that the suffering is undeserved. Such undeserved sufferings appeal to our sense of *injustice*." For this very reason, they arouse our pity. For Shakespeare (in *Richard III*), pity is an expression of our humanity and modulates the bestial in us: "No beast so fierce but knows some touch of pity." And Yeats (in "The Pity of Love") locates pity in the deepest recesses of love: "A pity beyond all telling / Is hid in the heart of love."

Yet pity is a tricky business. "Pity" is often used synonymously with "compassion," but they have different connotations. Compassion points to identification—feeling with. What is happening to you has happened to me; I know how you feel; I've been there. As Aristotle noted, pity presumes that what has happened to you *could* happen to me, but so far it hasn't. There but for good fortune go I. But we have had different fortunes. So pity sustains a tension between identification and differentiation, shared vulnerabilities and divergent fates.

We invariably prefer to be the pitier rather than the pitied. We worry that people expressing pity enjoy the secret satisfaction of superiority, perhaps even a subtle sadism. It is difficult to be the object of pity and not to feel diminished, not to feel pitiful, and we are put off by people we perceive as actively eliciting pity. There is a thin line between the evocation of pity and the manipulation of pity. As Jonathan Jeremiah Peachum, the sardonic entrepreneurial owner of "Peachum's Establishment for Beggars" in Brecht's *Threepenny Opera* declares: "There are a few things that'll move people to pity, a few, but the trouble is, when they've been used several times, they no longer work."

We often believe *self*-pity is inherently corrupted. The problem with self-pity is that it is a private arrangement, in which we are, at once, both the pitier and the pitied. While the capacity for pity (of others) is enriching, the state of being pitied verges always on degradation. In self-pity we play both roles ourselves. This makes the relationship between pity and self-pity a bit like the relationship between sex with someone else and masturbation. And we are generally uneasy with our tendencies toward self-indulgence. "Nobody believes his own misery," Peachum notes. "If you've got the stomachache and say so, it only sounds disgusting."

One feature of self-pity that makes it suspect is its close connection with implicit accusations toward others who have caused one's suffering. As with Ed's clocking his minutes in the cold outside my door, elaborating one's suffering sometimes operates to build a case against those at whose hands one has been disappointed and betrayed. Both in the real world and in one's own mind, power sometimes is granted to the victim. One common obstacle to the constructive use of psychotherapy is the need to make one's failures and deficits a monument to the (often real) failures of one's parents.

Yet the capacity for pathos toward oneself, the capacity to acknowledge and accept one's suffering as real and poignant and, sometimes, unjustified, is important and constructive. A sense of pathos represents a coming to terms with our relative helplessness in the face of many aspects of our lives. Side by side with Will's overwhelming guilt was his inability to be compassionate with himself concerning the limits of his own self-understanding in his first marriage. We came to realize that his childhood had not been so uniformly wonderful as he had remembered. The range of what he could allow himself to feel and know about himself had been truncated, and the marriage vows he had made in good faith had been made in ignorance of his own passionate qualities, which were later to emerge and take him by surprise. He still had many regrets. Will's growing compassion for himself about his situation did not erase his guilt, but it helped him to become less stuck in his inability to bear his guilt.

I once worked with a middle-aged woman who had been anorectic as a teenager and still suffered from various somatic symptoms and hypochondriacal preoccupations. She had virtually no memories of her family life. We knew that something had gone terribly wrong, that her inability to eat expressed something about her sense of her family as unable to sustain and embrace life. But she had no idea what had happened. Several years before, in going through her parents' possessions, she had come across, with horror, a portrait painted of her when she was a child. The artist had since become famous and the painting was quite valuable, but she could not bear to look at it and returned it to the painter. The portrait had captured something of the pain of her childhood. As an adult, the act of giving away the portrait was equivalent to the internal act of turning away from a pain she had been unable to face as a child. What she could not bear to acknowledge and think about became transformed into physical pains and incapacities. A sense of pathos toward ourselves, a kind of self-sorrow, allows us to accept this kind of psychic self-portrait.

The Degradation of Pathos and Guilt

Both pathos and guilt appear in two forms. One version enriches us and is essential to psychological growth. In the other, we degrade these feelings into private, static arrangements we make with ourselves to close off new and therefore risky experiences. Genuine pathos entails a compassionate acceptance of suffering caused by events and forces outside our control. Without pathos, we delude ourselves into denying our finitude, our limitations, our mortality. But accepting the limited control we have over our own lives is difficult, and genuine pathos teeters always on the brink of what we might term "pitifulness": victimology and self-pity. In this arrangement, the reality of ourselves as objects of forces outside our control slides over into claims we make as victims who, like Peachum's beggars, actively plot to evoke pity—in this case, from ourselves.

Similarly, genuine guilt entails an acceptance of accountability for suffering we have caused others (and ourselves). Without genuine guilt, we cannot risk loving, because our terror of our own destructiveness is too great. Without genuine guilt, we cannot allow ourselves to enjoy successes and pleasure. Guilt needs to be distinguished from what we might term "guiltiness," perpetual payments in an internal protection racket that can never end. If genuine self-pity is hard to bear because it entails an acceptance of the limited control we have over our worlds, genuine guilt is hard to bear because it entails an acceptance of the limited control we have over ourselves. We hurt those we love, and the damage of the past, like time itself, is irreversible.

In genuine guilt and genuine pathos, we are not willfully *trying* to do anything. We observe ourselves and are moved to pity. We consider the consequences of our actions for others and are moved to guilt. There is nothing to be done with these feelings; nothing *can* be done. We bear them and move on, informed and enriched as we encounter our next experiences. Our multiplicitous nature allows us different self-states and points of view—sometimes at the same time, sometimes sequentially. I might feel a deep sorrow and grief about past betrayal by others, lost loves, abandonments, and disappointments, but remain open to successful loves and newly emerging opportunities. I might feel a deep regret and guilt about my past betrayals of others, but remain open to second chances and new possibilities.

In self-pity and guiltiness, in contrast, we *are* trying to do something, and that effort fixes us in a static position. In my role as victim, I am involved in moving myself to pity; in my role as guilty perpetrator, I am involved in buying myself exoneration. Because pathos and guilt make us feel so vulnerable, we perpetually seek to bring them under the control of our fantasied omnipotence. By making static, private arrangements with ourselves around self-pity and guilt, we close ourselves off from engaging with a world of other people in which the risks, as well as the potential rewards, are enormous.

Any full-bodied romantic passion is laced with both pathos and guilt. Pathos derives from what Carson McCullers suggests is the loneliness of the lover, who brings a history of longing to his current desire, a history that adds texture to, but can hardly be gratified in, the present. Guilt derives from the inevitable partial bad faith of the lover, whose love is always laced with aggression and fantasies of revenge. And narratives of romantic love threaten always to degrade into self-pity and guiltiness, since both pathos and guilt are hard to bear.

Pathos and self-pity, guilt and guiltiness are not just private feelings or states of mind. They also become modes of communicating our experiences to others. There is perhaps no better vantage point from which to distinguish between genuine pathos and guilt and their corrupted twins, self-pity and guiltiness, than that of the listener to accounts of suffering. Pathos and guilt make no claims on the listener; they convey a sense of painful growth, of vulnerabilities shared. Self-pity and guiltiness operate as subtle, or sometimes not so subtle, interpersonal coercions. The listener is nudged either into reassurance ("What you did really was not so bad"; "You are really not quite so damaged as you think you are") or into collusion ("You really do deserve blame and punishment for your sins"; "They really have done you in").

Part of what builds texture early in romantic relationships is telling the tales of past loves. There are always mutually seductive pulls: you *were* bad, but *I*, in contrast to previous lovers, will forgive you; you *were* done wrong, but *I*, in contrast to previous lovers, will save you. If love lasts over time, one inevitably begins to feel some sympathy for the villainized lovers of the past and becomes less eager to pardon or save than to encourage the containment of more authentic pathos and guilt.

There is a dignity about pathos and guilt in their genuine forms, which is what makes the blues such a powerful form of expression, both moving and ennobling. The blues is a genre of music in which has been cultivated a particularly American, deep and rich tragic sensibility. In the ironic stance so central to the blues, the singer takes himself seriously indeed, yet stops short of taking himself too seriously. As the cultural and music critic Stanley Crouch has put it, the "blues is fundamentally a music that fights self-pity and even holds it up to ridicule, the singer scorning all self-deceptive attempts at ducking responsibility for at least *part* of the bad state of affairs." It is the characteristic irony of the blues that allows us both to pity ourselves for our limited control over our own romantic fate without anointing ourselves as victims, and to hold ourselves accountable for our culpability in our fate without self-mortification. What is uncoerced and spontaneous in our responses to ourselves provides our deepest potential for living fully. In the words of the songwriter David Bromberg, "You've got to suffer if you want to sing the blues."

6

Control and Commitment
in Romantic Love

But it must *happen*. You can't do anything for it with your will. You always seem to think you can *force* the flowers to come out. People must love us because they love us—you can't *make* them.

—D. H. LAWRENCE

Freedom's just another word for nothing left to lose.

—KRIS KRISTOFFERSON

THE IDEA OF UNCONSCIOUS MENTAL PROCESSES is a bit of a jolt; Freud was certainly right about that. It seems totally obvious that our minds are transparent to ourselves, that we know what is *on* or *in* our minds at any given time, and that we make our choices about what to do, what to say, what to think, accompanied by an on-going surveillance of our mental processes. The transparency of our minds is almost as obvious as the flatness of the earth. But both ideas, as it turns out, are wrong. Or, more precisely, both ideas are sort of right, but within a very narrow perspective. As our vantage point broadens, we begin to appreciate a very different context for our local impressions.

The complexity of our minds perhaps becomes less startling when we consider the enormous intricacy of our brains, which are composed of 100 billion neurons, or nerve cells, which are connected with one another through 100 trillion synaptic connections, or bridges between brain cells. The number of possible links or associations among the different cells is truly astounding. It was only when researchers in the area of computer science called artificial intelligence began to design computers to perform some of the simple tasks that our brains perform regularly, such as visual recognition, that we began to realize just how complex the neural structure and wiring inside our heads must be. Yet the apparent simplicity and transparency of mind are no accident or mere mistake in reasoning. They are undoubtedly adaptive necessities, making it possible for us to navigate our world with a sense of continuity and agency.

The Unbearable Density of Experience

Consider a hypothetical social event like a crowded cocktail party with colleagues, both acquaintances and strangers, in attendance. Let us say I am accompanied by a friend of long standing, who knows me quite well. My friend and I are quickly engaged with various people and small groups, some of them approaching us, some of them approached by us, bouncing around like balls in a pinball game until we leave an hour or so later. I was in a happy, comfortable state of mind when I arrived, and I notice that I am departing in a different mood, slightly agitated and a bit blue. What has happened? I am not sure.

So my friend and I rehash the sequence of encounters in some detail. I have varying relationships of quite different types with the people I interacted with and also with those with whom I did not speak. There were people I sought out and wanted to make contact with for different reasons; there were people I was not interested in speaking with. With some of those I had glancing conversations;

others I avoided by never making eye contact. I was aware of many people in the room, some of whom, in varying degrees, seemed to be seeking me out, some of whom, in varying degrees, seemed to be avoiding me. I was monitoring and processing information very rapidly, both about acquaintances and about strangers. Who were these people? What was my history with them? How were they presenting themselves to me now? What did I want with them? How was I experiencing myself speaking with them? How were they responding to me? I made many, many choices in the course of the hour, but it all went by so fast that I certainly did not have time to deliberate about what I was doing.

As my friend and I go over the details of the interactions, I begin to appreciate just how much was going on that was not in my conscious awareness at the time. There was the fellow I felt happy to see and eager to talk to, and the fellow I felt somehow stung by. There was the woman I found it fun to meet and talk to and the woman I found irritating and unsettling. What was it about each of these people that contributed to my response? Why did I react to those I did not know in the ways I did? Was it something they said or did? Was it what I had heard about them? Was it that they reminded me of other people I know? Was it what I knew about whom they associated with? As I begin to unpack the complexity of my thoughts and feelings about various people, I become aware of how many different intentions, inhibitions, hopes, and anxieties intersected with how many unarticulated memories, speculations, and anticipations.

The input from my friend becomes important. She has her own observations about these encounters. At points, I seemed to have been responding to things that she noticed without my realizing it. And she picked up some nuances in my self-presentation that had been lost on me. She had previously heard me telling some of the stories I told at the party, but tonight I delivered them in different ways with different people. Did they betray an easiness with some? A desire to impress others? At some points I said things, or became silent, in ways that struck her as a bit surprising, revealing facets of me she had not previously seen.

I begin to track my shifting moods. I realize that in one interaction I was taking a risk in a way that I felt was unreciprocated. In another I felt crowded by someone's overture to me. At one point I felt delighted by a sense of connection; at another I was unexpectedly intrigued, wanting more. Through this conversation, I slowly begin to map the shifts in my mood onto the process and fate of these interactions. Some connections seem pretty compelling, but there are plenty of unexplained nuances, a sense of more meanings than I can quite gain access to.

This hypothetical exploration of what happened during that hour at the cocktail party might continue for a long, long time. In fact, it would be potentially endless. So far I have been focusing only on my participation at the party and my friend's take on that. Before long we would need to explore the differences between her take and my take and the ways in which her perceptions grew out of the complexity of her relationships with all these people and with me. We would begin to wonder how much of what we thought was going on really *was* taking place. Did we invent some of the nuances and interpretations because we found them pleasing? And we would have to consider the complexities of *our* relationship and the ways they affected our behaviors and experiences at the party and our reflections about it now. Our understandings at any moment would be influenced by what was happening between us *at that very moment,* which in the subsequent moments we would begin to unpack. But of course the complex textures of the unpacking interaction between us would in turn require yet more unpacking.

Far from being transparent to myself, I understand myself always in contexts that are to varying degrees necessarily opaque and hidden from me. Trying to view and grasp myself completely at any point is a little like trying to outrun my shadow on a sunny day!

We are constantly making choices. But are they really choices? Some of the things I did at the party I did with an awareness of what I was doing. Other things I did with only a vague, unarticulated sense of my own agency. And there were other moves I made of which I was completely oblivious until my friend pointed them out to me. Are these all choices? They seem to be. But are they *my* choices? Who else's could they be? With some of them, as I become aware of what I did, I can report precisely *why* I did what I did, how it made perfect sense even though I was unaware of doing it at the time. This kind of choices Freud called "preconscious"—they were not in my awareness, but they were capable of becoming conscious once I noticed them or they were pointed out to me.

Preconsciousness operates in very much the same way as visual perception. We tend to assume we see a fairly wide swath of our visual world quite clearly, perhaps about 150 degrees in front of us, from our peripheral vision on one side to our peripheral vision on the other. But look closely ahead of you and notice how small a sector of the visual field you actually are seeing with clarity—perhaps two or three degrees. The rest of what we tend to assume we are seeing is actually quite fuzzy. We think we are seeing it clearly, and we keep track of it by shifting our vision back and forth periodically, assuring ourselves it in fact looks as we assume it looks. We are capable of seeing the rest of our visual field clearly by focusing our attention on it, but we don't in a continuous way. Preconscious meanings and choices operate similarly. We pursue many of our activities in the world on the basis of preconscious, blurry, fuzzy choices made without articulation and clear-sightedness but accessible to deliberation if we try.

Consider another possibility. Let us say one of the partygoers whom I did not know looks a great deal like a close relative of mine from childhood, an older cousin perhaps, whom I loathe, or whom I once loved, or both. Let us say that many years ago she spurned my love, and I dealt with my hurt feelings by deciding I was repelled by her. Remembering her now stirs up feelings of hatred, unrequited longing, and rejection that make me acutely uncomfortable. So I've become adept at not remembering her. In fact, I virtually never think of her. If I do, I tell myself how much I despise her; after a while I lose all memory of ever having loved her. But this woman at the party is a dead ringer for my lost object of desire. I glimpse her from afar and something stirs in me, but I am too occupied with other concerns to notice. I navigate my way through the party making choices that enable me to avoid this ghost from my past. But I don't realize I am doing this. If asked, I would deny it. I don't like thinking that my cousin could possibly still be so important to me that memories of her would affect my social behavior now. And I would find it unimaginable that my love for her might still be alive enough and feel dangerous enough to me that I would make choices with it in mind (although not in the part of my mind I have direct access to). These are mental processes and choices that Freud termed "unconscious." They are not only not in my awareness; they are not welcome. I (again without realizing it) actively bar them from awareness and don't recognize such thoughts as *mine* if presented with them.

We have been engaged in a hypothetical experiment in *self-consciousness,* imagining the sort of self-exploration that would be required to track the ways we operate with one another with complex, manifold intentions of three different sorts: some with deliberative self-awareness, some without our focal attention but recognizable as consistent with our conscious approach to living, and some unrecognizable to and disclaimed by our conscious agency. Isn't it fortunate that using our minds does not require such focal attention, such laborious self-consciousness? That could only be paralyzing. The complexity and efficacy of our activities require that we generate many of our intentions not just consciously but also preconsciously and unconsciously. So our subjective sense that our intentions and the meanings of our activities are all transparent is an effective illusion that makes our more or less seamless experience possible. Suddenly becoming aware of the complexity and multiplicity of our intentions would plunge us into the plight of the fabled centipede who, when asked how he manages to coordinate his one hundred legs when he walks, is instantly paralyzed by confusion. Preconscious and unconscious mental processes—these ideas seem so improbable and mysterious at first. But such processes are natural and inevitable consequences of the enormously complex lives our astounding brains make it possible for us to have.

Driver or Driven?

Talking about unconscious intentions or unconscious will is a bit peculiar, oxymoronic, a contradiction in terms. The terms "intention" and "will," in their ordinary usage, imply consciousness, deliberation, self-reflective choice. Yet psychotherapists regularly deal with choices, like the ones at our hypothetical party, that are made with only a minimal, or in many cases a complete, lack of any conscious sense of choosing. Who is the choosing agent? Is it *me*? Something *inside* me? A *part of* me? Although psychotherapists explore these processes all the time, nobody has developed a clear and graceful way to understand and speak about unconscious intentions. Doing so remains a problem for all of us.

The nature of human agency became problematic for us largely through Freud's contribution to the decentering of the individual within his own mind. Surely, before Freud, poets (such as Shakespeare, Goethe, Dostoevsky, and Tolstoy) and philosophers (such as Schopenhauer and Nietzsche) had pointed to motives operating within human experience of which the agent himself was unaware. But Freud expanded on these insights and developed a method— free association—for systematically exploring unconscious experience. And, most important, Freud portrayed us to ourselves in a fashion radically different from our customary self-appraisal. Rather than regarding unconscious motives as a pathological aberration, the exception, Freud came to understand unconscious intentions as the rule. We are driven, Freud wanted to show us, by dark forces unknown to ourselves. Not only are we not in complete charge; we often do not seem to have a clue about what is really going on. With his discovery of unconscious motivation, Freud exposed the illusory nature of man's claim to be master in his own house, in control of his own mind.

The concept of unconscious motivation is still a shock, quite foreign to many people, but in one way or another Freud's vision has seeped into the way we experience ourselves today, often in the form of doubt about our control over ourselves. Consider how quaint and pollyannaish seems the righteous claim to self-regulation among Freud's contemporaries: "I am the master of my fate / I am the captain of my soul," intoned the poet William Ernest Henley, crippled by tuberculosis of the bone but undaunted. Only the weak have lost control over their own experience, Henley is suggesting. But belief in the Victorian, Enlightenment-based ideal of an omnipotent, autonomous willpower, overseeing and in control of a mind transparent to itself, has generally faded. It reappears from time in slogans, political (as in Nancy Reagan's "Just Say No") and commercial (as in Nike's "Just do it!"). But the "just" in these slogans is a form of magical denial that the powerful physiological and psychological grip of drug addiction and deficits in athletic constitution and training can all be overcome by simple exertion of the will.

The other end of the continuum, the opposite of the traditional belief in the omnipotent will, is the doctrine of passive victimization, in evidence in television spectacles in which perpetrators of heinous crimes exonerate themselves by revealing their own past victimization. Not only are we not in control, they seem to be saying, we are pawns of what was done to us in our distant personal pasts. Psychotherapy is often misused in the service of this sort of self-exoneration.

Most us of struggle to understand ourselves in terms somewhere in between Henley's grandiose, omnipotent proclamations and the contemporary murderer's pleas of helplessness. Like me, trying to understand my actions and experiences at the hypothetical cocktail hour: there are some things I am up to that I know about clearly, others about which I am only dimly aware, and others about which I seem to be completely in the dark. So whether we have articulated it to ourselves or not, we all struggle with how to grasp and speak about our unconscious intentions. Considering Freud's efforts with these problems gives us some clues to our options.

If the individual does not control his own psyche the way, say, a driver controls his car, who does? Freud dethroned the naive belief in an omnipotent will steering a transparent and pliable mind—what looked like a driver (the conscious aspect of mind) became a cardboard dummy—but doing so left him with a problem that psychoanalysis has been struggling with ever since. Is the psyche really *out* of control, lurching this way and that? Or is there a remote control, a hidden controller inside the mind, unknown to the merely titular owner?

In the many concepts and metaphors he generated for thinking about mind, Freud went back and forth on this question. Very early on in some of his case descriptions, Freud imagined a secretly defiant "counter-will" as a kind of saboteur generating unconscious conflicts and troublesome symptoms. But in his later formal, "metapsychological" theorizing, Freud rejected the term "subconscious" (though this term is still often used in pop psychology writings) precisely because it implied an alternative consciousness operating in hidden recesses of the mind. Unconscious thoughts are not organized into a single subjectivity or perspective, Freud argued; they are fragmentary and dispersed.

But the tension in Freud's struggle to visualize a decentered mind remained. In 1923 he introduced the concept of the "id" as the repository of instinctual drives and the core of the unconscious. At times the id has qualities of an "it" (the literal translation of "id"), a kind of perverse, hidden imp that drives the psyche according to its own secret agenda. (This was the original meaning intended by Georg Groddeck, from whose *Book of the It* Freud borrowed the term.) And Freud at times pictured the relationship between the ego and the id as like the relationship between a rider and his horse. The horse, as anyone who has ridden horses well knows, operates as a powerful "counter-will." But at other times Freud portrays the id as diffuse and fragmentary, a "seething cauldron," or as like the ocean itself, the Zider Zee, which civilization slowly exposes, organizes, and brings under control.

Thus in dethroning the Enlightenment/Victorian ideal of an autonomous, omnipotent willpower, Freud created a conceptual vacuum in our ways of imagining our own minds, a vacuum which his subsequent images and metaphors of "the unconscious" never quite succeeded in filling. And neither have his descendants. Is the mind run by a hidden controller? Or is the sense we have of ourselves as individuals, as "selves," with an individually grounded coherence and agenda, completely illusory?

Post-Freudian theorists have tended to gravitate to one position or the other. And the different approaches to this issue have come to define some of the fundamental schisms in contemporary thought, both within and beyond psychoanalysis.

On the one hand, within some currents of American psychoanalysis there has been a restoration of a psychic center. In Freudian ego psychology, the reigning psychoanalytic ideology in the United States from the 1940s through the 1970s, the "ego" was granted many more powers and resources than Freud ever had in mind. Whereas Freud's ego was essentially a mediator, scurrying around at the interface between the id and external reality attempting to negotiate their very different aims, the ego of Freudian ego psychology has a powerful agenda of its own, synthesizing, adapting, and creating what Erik Erikson termed "identity."

On the other hand, within many currents of fashionable postmodern thought influenced by French post-structuralism, the philosophizing of Michel Foucault, and the theorizing of the well-known French psychoanalyst Jacques Lacan, there has been a complete obliteration of any meaningful sense of agency, psychic center, or coherent self. The persons we take ourselves to be, in this view, are merely "discursive" positions, inventions of language and cultural images.

This controversy has enormous significance for any attempt at understanding the nature of romantic passion. Is romantic love something we can will to develop and intend to maintain? When we are tired of it or distressed by it, can we will or intend romantic love to diminish or to cease altogether? Or if romantic love is outside our conscious, willful control, is it initiated, run, and terminated by some sort of hidden agent, a subconsciousness within us? Are there multiple intentions, dispersed motives, that converge to determine our romantic feelings? Or alternatively, might we regard powerful emotional experiences like romantic love as generated out of some combination of conscious agency and unconscious motives? If "I" give my love to you, what exactly am I giving and who is the "I" making the offering, and who, by the way, are *you*?

The Will

All major explanatory theories of human experience, both sociological and psychological, provide what philosophers have termed "grand narratives." They tell us what life is *really* about, what *really* drives our experiences. They are therefore necessarily reductive and deterministic. Each strives to expose underlying causes beneath the detailed surface level of human experience. Thus Marx attempted to demonstrate the impact of economic, social class interest on values, worldview, and all other features of personal life. Freud attempted to trace the guiding power of infantile sexual and aggressive wishes in adult emotional life. And a very different sort of psychology, "behaviorism," promoted by B. F. Skinner, tracks current choices back to the subject's past history of reinforcement. Virtually all sociologies and psychologies are deterministic in that they view human experience and behavior as products of forces (or motives) impinging upon the person; the content of the particular theory supplies the content of the motives. Choice, or the will, tends to be regarded as illusory. We think we are deciding what to do, but the choice is already determined by whatever causal forces (economic interest, infantile wishes, past reinforcements) are regarded as definitive according to the tenets of the particular theory.

What determined the moves I made at the cocktail party? A Marxist would be looking at my class history and the social and economic significance of the party and the other partygoers, assuming my unknowing choices were expressing and defending a class ideology and its interests. A Freudian would be busy detecting the ways in which the sequence of social encounters represented childhood scenarios and fantasied dramas, my reactions to them expressing infantile sexual and aggressive wishes and defenses against them. A behaviorist would be analyzing my actions in terms of recurrent patterns of behavior exposing my learned responses and past history of reinforcement. The one thing they would all agree on would be that whatever *I* thought I was up to at the party was a kind of benighted fairy tale, concealing the real motives and causes at work.

The exception to this general obliteration of the person as agent of his or her own experience has been existential philosophies and psychologies like those of Heidegger and Sartre. Here there is a great emphasis on choice, personal authenticity, and determination of one's fate, together with consequent guilt and angst. The problem here is that we are regarded as so self-determining, almost omnipotently so, that the limiting impact of our history, our childhood, and our preconscious and unconscious motivations is not taken into account. In fact, Sartre argued passionately that the concept of an "unconscious" was incoherent, a self-deceiving "bad faith." In this view, I revealed myself at the cocktail party, if I can stand being fully honest with myself, as an ingenious social operator, carrying out multiple, simultaneous agendas in a knowing fashion—including those, for example, regarding the woman whose resemblance to my cousin I pretended to be unaware of.

Anyone working as a psychotherapist or psychoanalyst struggles daily with the problem of reconciling these two perspectives, one illuminating various out-of-awareness motives for our behavior, the other reminding us that we, and not some dark and impersonal forces, are the ultimate agents of our own experience. No theorist has managed to systematically elaborate their confluence, but clinicians work this out in a rough-and-ready fashion all the time. We don't have to agree with Sartre that we are always completely transparent to ourselves to hold on to the sense that what we think we are up to has some relation to what we are actually doing!

Let's return to the cocktail party to see how this works. As noted earlier, the many different "choices" I made at the party fall into different categories with regard to how much of a self-conscious agent I experienced myself to be. At times I seemed to know just what I was up to; we might say that at those points my will was in the foreground of my experience. At other times I experienced myself as swept along by the flow of the party, making specific moves without much deliberation. When reflecting on them subsequently, I can provide reasons for those moves. I wasn't thinking things through, but I had a vague idea of what I was up to; we might say that at those points my will was in the background of my experience. And then there were those points which I was able to reconstruct afterward, with the help of my friend, when I was apparently operating in terms of a childhood conflict to which I was totally oblivious. I thought I knew what I was up to, but I was operating in some sense at odds with myself. We might say that at those points there was, in addition to my conscious will in the foreground, unconscious willing behind the scenes. In this way of approaching these matters, all activities, all choices necessarily reflect both motives (or reasons) and will, either in the foreground (consciously), in the background (preconsciously), or behind the scenes (unconsciously).

Which of these is the best place for the will to be? It depends. Many years ago I taught people to play tennis. There is no way to learn to play that game with any degree of proficiency without considerable self-consciously willed discipline. Throw the best natural athlete in the world a tennis racket and tell him to improvise, and he will only get so far. Instruction is necessary: grip the racket this way for the forehand, that way for the backhand; stand perpendicular to the net; support your weight on the balls of your feet; keep your eye on the ball; start your backswing just so; meet the ball this way for top spin, that way for a flat shot, this way for underspin; follow through in this fashion; keep your weight moving forward as you make impact with the ball; and so on. While you are learning the game, there is, necessarily, a great deal of willing operating in the foreground.

Once one becomes proficient at tennis, once the strokes have become patterned and fluid, the will recedes into the background. Self-conscious thought can get in the way. This sort of seamless performance is now fashionably referred to as the "zen" of tennis, but tennis players have for decades spoken of hitting ground strokes "in the groove," as if the racket were following a trajectory that is not intended and shaped but already laid out. And athletes in many sports suggest the lack of a subjective sense of agency when playing extremely well in phrases like "in the zone" or "out of one's mind." Of course, hitting three or four backhands into the net requires a call to the will to emerge once again into the foreground: to check grip, footwork, follow-through, momentum, and so on.

Thus for some activities, like playing tennis well, making love, sharing emotional intimacies, the will usefully hovers in the background. For other activities, like learning to play tennis, correcting wayward strokes, and learning about each other as a prelude to sharing sexual and emotional intimacies, intention and focus are crucial and the will often plays a necessarily foreground role. Many of our difficulties in living stem from the misapplication of the will. Some experiences, like intimacy, joy, or exhilaration, are possible only when the will has receded into the background; we get into trouble when we try, grandiosely, to self-consciously coerce those experiences. Other experiences, like really getting to know another person or disentangling interpersonal conflicts, require a fore-ground will and plenty of focal intention; we get into trouble when we try, naively, to simply "go with the flow" and hope for the best. Most practicing psychotherapists soon discover that the traditional psychoanalytic interpretation of motives must be complemented by an appreciation of the will if the therapy is not to degenerate into an exercise in post hoc explanations. On the one hand, the explication of motives without recognition of the complicity of the will, either actively or passively, leaves the *person* out of the explanation and hence encourages a self-serving and obfuscating bad faith. On the other hand, a focus on the will without setting it in the context of the motives and circumstances within which it is operating portrays the person as an impossibly omnipotent operator of a mind wholly transparent to itself.

Choice and the Erotic

Popular culture tells us that "chemistry" is crucial in love. There is nothing less agentic than chemistry. The excitement is either there or not there, we are told. The very purpose of chemistry as an explanatory principle serves to highlight the futility of intention, the irrelevance of the will in matters of love. However, a closer look at chemistry often reveals an approving will hovering in the back-ground, and a closer look at a lack of chemistry often reveals unconscious willing operating behind the scenes.

Fred began one session by expressing puzzlement at his own behavior. Among the reasons for which he had entered psychoanalytic treatment a year earlier was the almost complete lack of sexual contact between him and his wife. He understood this as deriving largely from her fear of sex; she had been raped as a teenager. She had little interest in sex for long stretches of time and always left it up to him to take the initiative. He experienced her response as a tepid compliance and had lost interest. The chemistry was gone and it was her fault. Yet Fred was aware of constrictions in his own emotional life and felt that he might also play a part in their problems.

Over the course of the year's work, we had explored important issues and the intimacy between Fred and his wife had opened up and deepened in several major respects. Yet sex remained virtually nonexistent. The evening before this session, Fred's wife had made a tentative overture which he had declined. He experienced her tentativeness as anti-erotic and off-putting, the very quality that had extinguished his desire. Yet when he thought about it afterward he realized that her overture had probably been very difficult for her; he had declined what might have been a movement in the direction of precisely the sort of intimacy he longed for.

For a psychoanalyst, Fred's puzzlement about himself, his sense that he seemed to be operating at cross-purposes, was a precious development, a very satisfying outcome of a year's work. We might say it was an opening into a sense of himself as decentered; he is not simply the rational, controlling agent of his own experience; there is more going on. And in many sessions in the months that followed we explored features of his experience that had bearing on his choice that night.

Fred declined his wife's overture because he was waiting for something else to happen—a sexual display from her that would be dramatic, expressive, unmistakable, and bold. Her tentativeness betrayed her conflict, and he was fearful of responding to something that might soon vanish. What if he reconnected with the intense desire he had felt for her in the early days of their relationship?

Could he bear the pain of losing their intimacy if she retreated once again? Could he control the rage that her possible future withdrawal might arouse in him? Her tentativeness signaled the absence of any guarantee against the riskiness, the endangerment he felt about his own desire and possible disappointment.

In another vein, her tentativeness resonated for Fred with his experience of his mother, who, during his childhood, oscillated between periods of vitality and exuberance and bouts of depression and withdrawal. He had become adaptively accustomed as a child to a wary emotional distance from his mother. He had renounced the moments of exhilaration to protect himself from the searing loneliness he felt at her withdrawals. Fred had similarly accustomed himself to a renunciation of sex with his wife that had become familiar, almost comfortable. Despite his longings, he began to realize, he was fearful of disturbing that renunciatory equanimity.

What if Fred's wife actually had made the kind of approach he longed for? What would that have been like? Along that line of exploration, we discovered that Fred's experience of sex, even at its best, was complex and conflicted. Sex at its most passionate felt "animalistic" and a bit sadistic. His most exciting lovers were women for whom he had little respect and regard; he tended to become devoted, as an asexual savior, to women he held in high regard. He experienced love as a worshipful conscientiousness; he experienced passion as a kind of reckless exploitation. Fred began to understand that although he longed for a fully expressive, unrestrained sexual intimacy with his wife, the unresolved tension in his experience of love and aggression and their confluence in desire made it difficult for him to imagine having such passionate intimacy with her without also losing her.

Another element of what was at stake for Fred in his rejection of his wife's overture came to light several months later. Fred's father had been orphaned as a teenager and had a stereotypical, almost caricatured masculine style, macho and withdrawn. But the father's distant demeanor would crack on rare occasions, often at extended-family events when he had been drinking. He would then speak tearfully about his fantasies of an impossible reunion with his parents, and Fred had a strong feeling of connection with him in a sense of isolation and longing he felt they shared. As invariably happens in psychoanalysis, key features of his relationships with others began to appear in his relationship with me. There was often a warm quality between us that I experienced as deepening over time, as we worked through various issues related to trust and anxiety. However, Fred found my professional approach to our work, which he appreciated, also off-putting, as if I, like his father, were remote and hiding from him the emotional places in which I really lived. And Fred began to search for fragments of information about what might be my secret pain, the longings I must be hiding from him and everyone else.

These imaginings of his, some of which were more accurate than others, surfaced in our work over two years, and I began to notice changing feelings in myself about them. Earlier our exploration of his fantasies about and perceptions of my hidden emotional recesses had felt vibrant and important to me. As my fondness for Fred grew, though, I began to find annoying his conviction that what actually took place between us was less real than his imagined connection with my pain. So I began to point to ways in which an imagined intimacy through private suffering served to undo real intimacy that might develop. This exploration of a search for intimacy resulting in distancing between us proved very useful and, it soon became apparent, served as an analogue to the way Fred positioned himself with his wife. He loved his wife deeply and longed for a more open closeness, sexual and otherwise, with her. And he was certain, almost, that she also loved him deeply and experienced a similar poignant longing. Such a longing was the most intense imaginable feeling for him, like the longing he glimpsed at rare moments in his father. We came to understand that Fred's experience of himself and his wife, longing for each other in a perpetually frustrated state, was his ideal of the most intimate relatedness possible. Actual sex between them could only result in a falling off, a diminution of that exquisite, complementary longing which locked them together. Thus he felt he would have much more to lose than to gain in reciprocating his wife's sexual approach.

Any productive analysis generates endless motives and meanings. Psychodynamic interpretations are infinite. The question is: How do they bear on Fred's struggle for self-understanding and a more satisfying life? Where is *Fred* in the middle of all of this?

Surely Fred was not the pre-Freudian agent of Victorian times, with total command over a transparent self. Yet Fred was clearly operating with an agenda, or, rather, several different agendas, with different degrees of self-awareness. Fred was actually in several different, conflictual places within his own experience at the same time. Fred was a fearful, cynical, self-regulating agent, tamping down what he saw as his own ravenous desire and lethal destructiveness; Fred was a devoted and loving agent, preserving his ties to his mother in her depression and his father in his strangulated, secret longings; and Fred was a self-protective agent, guarding the intensity of his own longings as the deepest, most precious thing about himself.

Fred, like most of us, aspired to an ideal, sentimentalized sexuality, an abandonment without risk. But sexuality is, by its very nature, fraught with uncertainty, complexity, and vulnerability. Sexual passion is inevitably accompanied by self-discovery: dependency, disappointments, and aggression. And sexual passion is inevitably accompanied by other-discovery: the necessary implications of granting another the power to arouse, satisfy, and disappoint. This is why, for many couples, sex becomes routinized and boring over time. It is not that familiarity breeds lack of interest, but that as mutual dependencies deepen, as shared lives become more complexly intertwined, sexual passion, with all its accompanying risks, becomes increasingly dangerous.

Thus we are perpetually attempting to expand our will into a total control, to wrap the tendrils of our fantasied omnipotence around areas of experience in which we feel vulnerable and at risk: sexual excitement, enthrallment, dependency, rage, pathos, and guilt. Fred learned that the choice he made that night, seemingly at odds with himself, was a choice made for many reasons, based on beliefs he had come by honestly and feelings he had learned, through painful experiences, to fear. An important aspect of his eventual capacity to make other choices was a growing ability to experience himself as, in fact, the always incompletely self-aware constructor of his world.

What about chemistry? Are romantic and sexual excitement, then, completely voluntaristic? One cannot manufacture feelings, with all the will at one's disposal. There is a delicacy and complex contingency to both love and hate. One cannot make them happen, and one cannot will their resuscitation once they have expired. And yet deep love and hate, in contrast to fleeting attractions and antipathies, cannot be sustained unless one *wants* to keep loving and hating. I am speaking of willing here not only in the simple conscious sense but also in a fashion that is often in the background (preconscious) or behind the scenes (unconscious). A commitment is required to sustain lovers worthy of continued devotion as well as enemies worthy of continued malice. The anguished persons who claim to love or hate unwillingly, despite themselves, are aware only of the conscious version of themselves, while they love or hate on behalf of another version of themselves that is operating behind the scenes.

Are You in Love?

Charles had been in analysis for several years. His relationships with women had become depressingly redundant. He found not being in a relationship intolerable and repeatedly became obsessed with the hunt for a girlfriend. He was adept at evoking women's interest and became easily infatuated, most often with someone remote or inaccessible. As the latest object of his desire became more interested in him, he would enter a thicket of dense ruminations about whether she was, in fact, the right woman for him, whether he really was excited by her and did love her. The more he ruminated, the less he felt for the woman and the more suffocated he became by her feelings for him. Toward the end of the cycle he longed for the escape that ending the relationship would provide, so that he could be free to hunt a variety of women once again. But almost as soon as he found himself unattached he would begin to court a new commitment.

Over several years of analysis, the futility of this pattern became increasingly clear to him; for periods of time he was able to suspend his obsessions about whether he felt enough for a particular woman and to actually have more authentic feelings for her. Then, when he had been with Sarah for almost a year, and with her had experienced some stretches of pleasurable intimacy, she confronted him. They were at the point in their relationship where, she felt, they should be telling each other, "I love you." She had said it several times, and he seemed to have withdrawn. So she had stopped saying it. Sarah, who struck me as a woman of considerable emotional maturity, was not interested in coercing protestations of love from Charles. But she felt that the lack of such verbal expressions of love was not unimportant and probably indicated a ceiling on what was possible in their relationship.

Sarah's confrontation created something of a crisis for Charles, and he, and then he and I, spent quite a bit of time trying to sort out exactly what he *did* feel about her in different situations. There were times, he noticed, when "love is in the air." I became intrigued about what this meant. These moments when love was in the air often followed intense shared experiences, such as engrossing conversations or exciting sex. The love that was in the air was a feeling that was clearly a product of the relatedness between them; but who, exactly, was feeling what?

The easiest way for Charles to approach this question was to assume that Sarah, not he, felt the love; he felt *her* feeling love for him, and therefore he felt pressured to declare a love he did not really feel. But, we came to understand, that description did not do justice to the situation. It was not easy for him to know what he felt because he felt so obliged to gratify and control what he imagined was her need for him (he fantasized about taking a polygraph test to discern what, in fact, he did feel). When he could free himself from his largely self-imposed pressure to say things he did not feel, he came to realize that he certainly did feel something for Sarah in these moments. But was it love? It had elements of warmth, dependency, gratitude, security, exhilaration. But was it love? *Does* the feeling of love come in a prepackaged form, waiting to be correctly identified and named? Or does the naming itself make it into love?

As we struggled to sort out his experience, it became apparent that with Sarah Charles had many of what we came to regard as the components of love: moments of closeness, connection, deep feelings. But to feel he was "in love" required that something be done with those components, a knitting them together into a commitment he would name as love. It is in that act of consolidation that the will plays an important part, either facilitating or obstructing a commitment to love. Chemistry certainly contributes to creating the components, but there is a choice, a commitment in loving, that cannot be reduced to its emotional ingredients. Without accepting responsibility for that choice, Charles, like many people, assumed that with the "right" woman he would someday simply find himself in love.

One could approach this situation via the traditional psychoanalytic concept of projection. Of course Charles loves Sarah, this psychoanalytic construct explains, but he is too anxious to allow himself that feeling. So he projects his love into her, experiences it as coming from her, and controls it *in* her by distancing himself from her. Love is "in the air" because that is where Charles projects it. I believe that there is some value in this formulation, but that it is also misleading. I came to feel that the love Charles felt *in* Sarah was not just his projection; it was not just a fantasy of his affect residing in her. She did seem to be feeling love for him at those moments. The more we explored the situation, the less useful was the effort to choose between the view that the love "in the air" was *hers* which he feared and the view that it was *his* which he exiled outside the boundaries of his experience of himself. We seemed to be speaking about a feeling that could exist only if it operated in both of them, an experience that *required* two participants to ignite and fuel. So, in an important sense, this feeling they had in relation to each other *was* "in the air"; it was not simply in one or both of them; it had a transpersonal quality, crossing the semipermeable boundaries between self and others, agents and their objects.

Yet there was an important difference between the ways Charles and Sarah were processing or organizing their feelings. Sarah wanted to say "I love you" and also wanted Charles to say this to her. The more Charles and I mulled over the implications of Sarah's wish, the clearer it became that saying "I love you" is not just a report on a prepackaged feeling, but also what linguists call a "performative." Telling someone "I love you" has, built into it, various other messages and actions. It says "I like loving you"; "I want to love you"; "I accept and embrace my loving you"; "I want to evoke an expression of what you feel for me." Saying "I love you" entails will, the emergence of Charles as a different sort of agent, committed to engaging Sarah in a more fully developed interpersonal event. It is self-reflectively self-defining and calls for a recognizing response from the other. Becoming that sort of agent required for Charles giving up more familiar versions of himself as a cynical, self- and other-controlling agent and, on a deeper level, a devoted agent, preserving his tie to his mother, who, he secretly suspected, wanted to keep him for herself, in union with her own depressive longings.

The relationships among affect, behavior, and language are enormously complex and contextual. The conventional pressure to say "I love you" often *does* have a coercive, deadening impact on relationships. What was crucial for Charles was to decide whether or not he wanted to enhance the vitality of his relationship with Sarah and to become the sort of agent who could do so, with all the attendant risks; if he did, he needed to find a way, with or without saying "I love you," to do so. In this sense, Sarah was right. When two people say "I love you" to each other (or something equivalent), they are not just reporting on what has happened but contributing to determining what sort of agents they can become for themselves and each other, determining whether and how their relationship may deepen and whether certain paths of development will be foreclosed.

Constructing Experiences and Commitments

All models of mind are based on metaphors; we can't really visualize mind without comparing it with something else. Freud drew on the physics and technology of his day for his mechanistic metaphors, in which mind is the product of hydraulic-like forces channeled by machine-like structures. The model of mind I favor is based on the comparison of mental processes with human activities like the building of a house or a sculpture. Critics of such constructivist models often argue that they lack a recognition of the role of psychic structure, the power of the past, and that they glorify a kind of Sartrean omnipotence: if I construct my mind rather than being determined by it, doesn't that imply that I can make it into anything I want? These criticisms can be addressed if we enter further into the metaphor of construction.

We have been thinking a lot about building sandcastles, but let us say that we are now interested in building a house, and the contracting company is The Three Little Pigs, Inc. One partner in the company builds with straw, one with sticks, and one with bricks. All three houses are constructed, and there is a wide range of design possibilities. However, the materials employed lend themselves to very different possibilities, and each offers very particular constraints. The houses are not determined by the materials, but the houses are constrained by the properties of the materials. Similarly, the marble Michelangelo used for sculpting his *David* did not determine the statue, but it certainly had both a facilitating and a constraining impact on the result. The statue would have looked quite different if it had been made out of clay, or iron, or Lego blocks. Houses and statues are constructed, but the materials out of which they are constructed constrain the possibilities.

Similarly, human experience is constructed—consciously, preconsciously, and unconsciously. It is constructed out of many experiential dimensions, perceptions, memories, imagination, available cultural images and mythologies, bodily sensations, and so on, all operating as psychic building materials. Each of those dimensions of our experience imposes constraints upon the range of what can be constructed, but none of them determines the result in a direct causal fashion.

Psychotherapists and their patients struggle to collaborate on a narrative of the patient's experience and of their experiences together. These narratives are themselves collaborative constructions, constructions of constructions. Analytic narratives explore, in an often painstaking fashion, the complex reasons for the analysands' choices—their motives—yet at the same time recognize the patients' role in making choices in the context of conscious and unconscious meanings. We exercise our will embedded in situations, the meanings of which we often only dimly grasp or, sometimes, are quite oblivious of. Much of the craft of the psychoanalyst lies in the collaborative discovery with the analysand of a voice that traces the operations of the will, through its varieties of agency, and that strives to hold the tension between the assumption of responsibility and the avoidance of moralistic blaming.

So the challenge for both Fred and Charles, as for Brett and Susan (Chapter 1), Harold, George, and Veronica (Chapter 2), Cathy and Carl (Chapter 3), Jake (Chapter 4), and Ed and Will (Chapter 5) is not simply to arrive at the perpetually illusory ultimate interpretation of their motives, but to find a way to connect with a sense of themselves, to experience themselves, as the agents of their motives, either willing those motives or else willfully insisting upon (and then disclaiming) them. The ultimate yield of self-understanding is less a *particular* understanding, the *correct* interpretation, than the emergence of a self-reflective form of experience which breaks through the closed circle of repetitive, self-defeating interpersonal relationships and sustains the tension between agency and unconscious motivation, in which willing perpetually shapes what may be opaque and fragmentary psychic processes into the complex, often surprising lives we lead.

Sandcastles for Two

Popular magazines offering advice to those wearily enduring long-term relationships provide many suggestions about things to *do* to improve them. Time might be better spent reflecting on what one is *already doing!* Spontaneity, as devotees of meditation learn over and over again, is discovered not through action but through refraining from one's habitual action and discovering what happens next. Desire and passion cannot be contrived. But desire and passion occur in contexts, and we have a good deal to do with constructing contexts in which desire and passion are more or less likely to arise.

It is much easier to discern our role in constructing contexts for commitment than to discern our role in constructing contexts for spontaneity. We tend to assume we are in omnipotent control of our commitments and to romanticize the uncontrolled in spontaneity. We build cities, inventing our environments, sometimes dangerously godlike, out of thin air, and then romanticize nature and wilderness as if (with kayaks and hiking shoes) we could simply encounter them raw and pristine. But in matters of love, deeper, more authentic commitments can be made and maintained only with an awareness of change and transformation outside our agentic control. Romantic commitments in love entail not a devotion to stasis but a dedication to process in the face of uncertainty. Genuine passion, in contrast to its degraded forms, is not split off from a longing for security and predictability, but is in a continual dialectical relationship with that longing. In order for romantic involvements to remain vital and robust over time, it is crucial that the commitment not be so rigid as to override spontaneity and that spontaneity not be so rigid as to preclude commitment.

The proliferating realities of the external worlds we inhabit are mirrored by the deepening complexities of our understanding of ourselves. We want and need many different things at once: dependability and surprise, having and longing, knowing and imagining. And in our passionate relationships we feel many things in rapid succession: desire, vulnerability, adoration, betrayal, hatred, pathos, guilt, and possibly renewal. But it is no simple matter to determine whether the firm stability we long for is reality, illusion, or delusion and whether castle-building draws one away from life or generates a domain within which a more vibrant, meaningful life can be created.

Central to the delicate paradoxes of romance is the longing for permanence and certainty that emerges from desire. The exhilaration of romantic passion generates claims for continuity and security that, if they are taken too seriously, can only snuff out the freedom and spontaneity that were the ground of the passion in the first place. "Time held me green and dying," said Dylan Thomas in *Fern Hill:* green and dying, alive but changing, growing yet disappearing, caught by the constraints of flux and temporality, but singing.

Romance in relationships is a sandcastle for two. It is a precondition for passion, but not a permanent abode. The sandcastles of romance demand, by their shifting nature, continual rebuilding. Passionate intimacy requires a multiplicity of connections that cannot be housed in a singular, steady arrangement. The inevitability of perpetual change over time, like Nietzsche's incoming tide, washes out all sandcastles and gives the lie to aspirations of permanence.

It is no wonder that the degradation of romance, the segregation of its different facets, is so common: the terra firma, the sense of stability and predictability we require, is often separated from the vagaries of castle-building, and romantic excitement is titrated through the vicarious passions of soap operas and celebrity-gazing. The popularity of self-help books on relationships expresses the deep, widespread longing for some sort of romantic Baedeker, a relationship map for distinguishing sand from more stable building materials, to resolve these tensions.

But romance in relationships is not cultivated through a resolving of tensions, the discovery of a secret, a labored struggle to contrive novelty. The cultivation of romance in relationships requires two people who are fascinated by the ways in which, individually and together, they generate forms of life they hope they can count on. It entails a tolerance of the fragility of those hopes, woven together from realities and fantasies, and an appreciation of the ways in which, in the rich density of contemporary life, realities often become fantasy and fantasies often become reality.

Notes

Introduction

21 Sigmund Freud, "A Difficulty in the Path of Psychoanalysis" (1917), *The Standard Edition of the Complete Psychological Works of Sigmund Freud* [henceforth SE] (London: Hogarth Press, 1953-1974), 17: 137–144.

22 hard for us to accept: Freud noted that each of these broadly wounding blows to human self-estimation was anticipated in some fashion: the cosmological blow by Pythagoras, the biological blow by the animism and totemism of non-Western cultures, and the psychological blow by the philosopher Schopenhauer.

23 to paraphrase Nietzsche: Nietzsche proclaimed in *Thus Spake Zarathustra:* "God is dead."

25 "omnipotence of thought": In *Totem and Taboo* Freud discovered omnipotence of thought in what, with the ethnocentricity customary in his day, he considered "primitive" (that is, non-Western) peoples and also in obsessional neurotics.

25 romance and its degradation: Precursors to some of the ideas developed in this book are to be found in earlier papers of mine: "Psychoanalysis and the Degradation of Romance," in *Storms in Her Head: Freud and the Construction of Hysteria,* ed. Muriel Dimen and Adrienne Harris (New York: Other Press, 2000).

25 many psychologists now consider it to be crucial: Heinz Kohut, through

what he called self psychology, effected a revolution in theorizing about narcissism and its place in normal and creative experience.

26 Isaiah Berlin, *The Roots of Romanticism* (Princeton: Princeton University Press, 1999), p. xiii.

29 Harold Bloom, *Shakespeare: The Invention of the Human* (New York: Riverhead Books, 1998).

1. Safety and Adventure

39 Jay Greenberg, *Oedipus and Beyond. A Clinical Theory* (Cambridge, Mass.: Harvard University Press, 1991).

39 Erich Fromm, *Man for Himself* (Greenwich, Conn.: Fawcett, 1947).

39 some historians date the emergence: D. de Rougemont, *Love in the Western World* (New York: Pantheon, 1956).

40 more fully sexualized: In *Romantic Longings: Love in America, 1830-1980* (New York: Routledge, 1991), the sociologist Steven Seidman traces "the progressive 'sexualization of love'": "Between the early part of the nineteenth century and the later part of the twentieth century, the meaning and place of sex in relation to love, and therefore the meaning of love, underwent important changes. Love changed from having an essentially spiritual meaning to being conceived in a way that made it inseparable from the erotic longings and pleasures of sex . . . The Victorian language of love as a spiritual communion was either marginalized or fused with the language of sensual desire and joy" (p. 4). In the middle-class Victorian culture in which Freud lived and wrote, Seidman argues, the importance of sex in marriage was cautiously acknowledged by popular advice writers, "provided it was moderate in its frequency and did not incite sexual desires" (p. 26).

40 R. Bellah, R. Madsen, W. Sullivan, A. Swidler, and S. Tipton, *Habits of the Heart: Individualism and Commitment in American Life* (New York: Harper and Row, 1985), pp. 89, 93.

41 fundamentally regressive and defensive: As we shall see in Chapter 3, Freud regarded what he termed the "overvaluation" of the beloved as a consequence of the projection of a segment of primary narcissism onto the other: the beloved is loved as perfect and complete, as the very small baby loves himself. Freud, *On Narcissism: An Introduction* (1914), SE 14:

67–102. Because it depleted the ego of its own narcissism, Freud considered idealization of the other to be immature and dangerous, and romance, therefore, to be inherently regressive.

Idealization, particularly as developed in the highly influential (Melanie) Kleinian psychoanalytic tradition, has been regarded as fundamentally a defense against destructive aggression. Because the idealization in romantic love is a bulwark against hate, in this view, love itself is unstable, developmentally primitive, and less preferable than a more ambivalent relationship to the object.

42   a background feature of American culture: See Leslie Fiedler, *Love and Death in the American Novel* (New York: Stein and Day, 1966).

42   Renunciation . . . was crucial: I have explored this dark era of American psychoanalysis in "The Psychoanalytic Treatment of Homosexuality: Some Technical Considerations," *International Review of Psychoanalysis* 8 (1981): 63–87.

44   stable and predictable structures: This is the central feature of self as traditionally understood within Freudian ego psychology, which was the dominant American psychoanalytic ideology from the 1950s through the 1970s. See, e.g., Edith Jacobson, *The Self and the Object World* (New York: International Universities Press, 1964); Otto Kernberg, *Internal World and External Reality* (New York: Jason Aronson, 1980).

44   a continuous, core self: This is the way the self is portrayed in Heinz Kohut's self psychology, which emerged from Freudian ego psychology in the 1970s and has had a profound influence on American psychoanalysis.

44   a kernel that . . . seeks validation: This is the way the self is portrayed in some versions of what is known as British object relations theory. See, e.g., Harry Guntrip, *Schizoid Phenomena, Object Relations and the Self* (New York: International Universities Press, 1969).

44   newer theoretical currents: See, e.g., Thomas Ogden, *The Primitive Edge of Experience* (Northvale, N.J.: Jason Aronson, 1989) and *Subjects of Analysis* (Northvale, N.J.: Jason Aronson, 1994); Irwin Hoffman, *Ritual and Spontaneity in the Psychoanalytic Process* (Hillsdale, N.J.: Analytic Press, 1998); Philip Bromberg, *Standing in the Spaces: Essays on Clinical Process, Trauma, and Dissociation* (Hillsdale, N.J.: Analytic Press, 1998); Donnel Stern, *Unformulated Experience: From Dissociation to Imagination in Psychoanalysis* (Hillsdale, N.J.: Analytic Press, 1997).

44   Adam Phillips, *On Flirtation* (Cambridge, Mass.: Harvard University Press, 1994), 41.

45 "secure attachment": See the groundbreaking work on early development by John Bowlby and Mary Ainsworth.

46 imprinted into the child's desire: Jean Laplanche, *Life and Death in Psychoanalysis* (Baltimore: John Hopkins University Press, 1976).

50 "giving something you don't have to someone you don't know": Jacques Lacan quoted in Phillips, *On Flirtation,* 39.

55 Harold Bloom, *Shakespeare: The Invention of the Human* (New York: Riverhead Books, 1998), 88.

2. *The Strange Loops of Sexuality*

61 a tragic waste of time: In earlier decades, American psychoanalysts became involved in trying to convince homosexual patients that their homosexuality was a defensive retreat from an underlying heterosexuality, which they should, through great effort, force themselves to establish. The results of this campaign were tragic. For an account of this unfortunate episode in the history of American psychoanalysis, see my "The Psychoanalytic Treatment of Homosexuality: Some Technical Considerations," *International Review of Psychoanalysis* 8 (1981): 63–87.

62 are actually their own constructions: See the wonderful chapter "Looking at Obstacles" in Adam Phillips, *Kissing, Tickling and Being Bored* (Cambridge, Mass.. Harvard University Press, 1993).

63 alone in the presence of another: See D. W. Winnicott, "The Capacity to Be Alone" (1958), in *The Maturational Process and the Facilitating Environment* (New York: International Universities Press, 1965).

64 Freud, drawing on Darwin: Freud lived and worked during the first great wave of the assimilation of the Darwinian revolution, which has affected virtually every dimension in which human beings have come to understand themselves. Although profoundly revolutionary in many ways, the Darwinism of Freud's day also carried forward the basic Platonic-Christian theme of stratification that had dominated Western culture for centuries, now in scientifically authoritative terms. For Plato, as for the Judeo-Christian tradition, we descended from above, falling into time from an eternal, paradisal world of purity and harmony.

64 fuel all the higher levels of the mind: Nesting stratifications within stratifications, Freud regarded sexuality in itself as layered. Oral, anal, and exhibitionistic interests were residues of the sexuality of subhuman species.

64   Freud, *Introductory Lectures on Psycho-Analysis* (1916–1917), SE 16: 311–312.

66   spiders spin spider webs: Steven Pinker, *How The Mind Works* (New York and London: W. W. Norton, 1997), p. 173.

69   "the most complex word in the language": P. Coates, *Nature: Western Attitudes since Ancient Times* (Berkeley: University of California Press, 1998), p. 1.

71   our nearest primate relatives: In *Chimpanzee Politics: Power and Sex among Apes* (Baltimore: John Hopkins University Press, 1989), Frans de Waal notes the irony of the former "Latin name for the chimpanzee: *Pan satyrus.* Among chimpanzees . . . mating occurs only when the female is in oestrus. As soon as her swelling decreases the males lose interest. There are also long periods when the female's cycle stops or is very irregular . . . this means that months can sometimes go by without any sexual inter-course at all between the adult animals" (pp. 156–157). And the sexual-ity of the bonobo, who along with chimpanzees are our closest genetic and evolutionary relatives, is hardly marked by the intense primitivity characteristic of some human sexuality: "Sexual encounters of the bonobo kind are strikingly casual, almost more affectionate than erotic." Frans de Waal and Frans Lanting, *Bonobo: The Forgotten Ape* (Berkeley: University of California Press, 1997), p. 5.

71   Douglas R. Hofstadter, *Godel, Escher, Bach: An Eternal Golden Braid* (New York: Basic Books, 1979).

74   the forms through which we experience it: See Judith Butler's incisive argument against the concept of the "natural" when applied to sexuality in *Bodies That Matter* (New York: Routledge, 1993).

76   Martin Heidegger, *Being and Time* (London: SCM Press, 1962).

76   Mobius strip: A Mobius strip is a surface with only one side, formed by giving a half-twist to a narrow, rectangular strip of paper and then pasting its two ends together.

78   Leslie Farber: Farber's trenchant essays, along with some insightful com-mentary, have recently been republished as *The Ways of the Will* (New York: Basic Books, 2000).

80   others whom we perpetually regenerate: One of the most important con-cepts in contemporary psychoanalytic thought is associated with the phrases "internal objects" and "internal object relations," referring to the way early significant relationships and experiences become internalized as

durable features of the individual's mind. We populate our inner, subjective, private world, our innermost sense of self, with early relationships and experiences, and we naturally anticipate that in our daily encounters with adult reality we will run into the same characters and situations. For more on internal object relations see Thomas Ogden, *The Matrix of the Mind* (Northvale, N.J.: Aronson, 1986); Stephen A. Mitchell, *Relational Concepts in Psychoanalysis* (Cambridge, Mass.: Harvard University Press, 1988).

80 linked with and shaped by . . . implicit others: The literary theorist and philosopher Elaine Scarry, in her study of torture, *The Body in Pain* (New York: Oxford University Press, 1985), argues that the physical experience of pain always becomes personified. Someone is doing this to us.

81 Poets, philosophers, and psychoanalytic theorists: See, e.g., the work of Georges Bataille, and Otto Kernberg, *Love Relations* (New Haven: Yale University Press, 1995).

81 the same thing in different forms: The psychologist Irene Fast introduced into contemporary gender theory a modern version of the Greek myth (from Plato's *Symposium*) that humans were once hermaphroditic, four-legged, double-genitaled creatures who were split apart. According to Fast, small children regard themselves as bisexual, each one containing, in potentia, all the attributes of both boys and girls. The recognition of gender differences, Fast believes, causes not so much a fear or sense of castration as a narcissistic blow to bisexual omnipotence. The very establishment of a sense of gender identity also establishes a sense of gender counter-identity. And, as postmodern theorists like Judith Butler have argued, gender is centrally defined and experienced negatively in terms of what one is not. According to Butler, masculinity is established by and *is* nothing more than the exclusion of the feminine, and femininity is established by and *is* nothing more than the exclusion of the masculine.

84 control we struggle to maintain over our lives: The linguist George Lakoff provides an interesting angle on these issues in *Women, Fire, and Dangerous Things: What Categories Reveal about the Mind* (Chicago: University of Chicago Press, 1990). Lakoff suggests that feelings, like all human experiences, are both embodied and imaginative. Our understandings of our feelings are, necessarily, based on metaphors, and our basic underlying metaphors are grounded in our physiology. Lakoff catalogued metaphors we use to describe and speak about powerful emotions like

lust: hunger ("He is sex-starved"; "She is quite a dish"); wild animals ("Don't touch me, you brute!"; "Hello, my little chickadee"); heat ("I've got the hots for her"); insanity ("I'm madly in love with him"); machines ("You turn me on"); games, sometimes deadly games ("I'm going to score tonight"; "She's dressed to kill"); war ("He's known for his conquests"); and physical forces ("I was knocked off my feet). Lakoff believes many of these metaphors derive from the physiology that mediates feeling states like lust and anger. Thus the rise in skin temperature and pulse rate and the antigravitational properties of tumescence all lend themselves to descriptions of lust (as well as anger) in metaphors of heat, energy, and physical forces. We might say that Freud took the implicit metaphors for lust embedded for centuries in our Western folk psychology and reified them into an actual instinctual force he called "libido," and then, circularly, derived our experiences of sexuality from that reified force.

85   relief from the strain of psychic structure itself: See Emmanuel Ghent's classic "Masochism, Submission, Surrender: Masochism as a Perversion of Surrender" (1990), in Stephen A. Mitchell and Lewis Aron, eds., *Relational Psychoanalysis: The Emergence of a Tradition* (Hillsdale, N.J.: Analytic Press, 1999).

87   what the fantasizers do *not* want to do: See Jessica Benjamin's rich contributions on the relationships between fantasy and reality, internal and external, past and present, in emotional relationships: *Bonds of Love: Psychoanalysis, Feminism, and the Problem of Domination* (New York: Pantheon, 1988); and *Like Subjects, Love Objects* (New Haven: Yale University Press, 1995). In the latter she argues against the claim, made in many quarters, that pornography reflects what its consumers secretly desire most to do; rather, she suggests, pornography often provides a safe venue for excitement precisely because it is at a remove from actual relationships.

3. Idealization, Fantasy, and Illusions

93   three states of mind: When I presented a version of this chapter in Toronto, the psychoanalyst Sam Stein pointed out that whatever the ontological status of the sandcastles, the psychoanalyst collects the rent!

98   less an expression of rationality than of faith: In *Kissing, Tickling and Being Bored* (Cambridge, Mass.: Harvard University Press, 1993), Adam Phillips writes of Freud's devotion to science as a form of idolatry.

99　Audrey Richards: story told in Nathaniel Branden, *The Psychology of Romantic Love* (New York: Bantam, 1983).

100　According to some historians: See Philippe Ariès, *Centuries of Childhood: A Social History of Family Life* (New York: Vintage, 1962).

101　"the general feeling"; "she could disappear": Ariès, *Centuries of Childhood,* pp. 38, 128.

102　For this comparison between Romanticism and the Enlightenment, I am drawing on Isaiah Berlin's brilliant *The Roots of Romanticism* (Princeton: Princeton University Press, 1999). Quotation from p. 67.

103　epistemological foundational security: One of the most important of Richard Rorty's enormously influential contributions to contemporary philosophy has been his critique of this longing and the problems it has generated. See his *Philosophy and the Mirror of Nature* (Princeton: Princeton University Press, 1979), and *Objectivity, Relativism, and Truth* (Cambridge: Cambridge University Press, 1991).

105　exploring different sorts of problems: Thomas Kuhn's *The Structure of Scientific Revolutions* (Chicago: University of Chicago Press, 1962), in which he introduced this new perspective on science, has had a powerful impact on the history and philosophy of the social sciences as well as the natural sciences.

105　Hans Loewald, "Psychoanalysis as Art and the Fantasy Nature of the Psychoanalytic Situation" (1974), in Loewald, *Papers on Psychoanalysis* (New Haven: Yale University Press, 1980), p. 368.

106　brought alive through fantasy: Heinz Kohut, in, e.g., *The Restoration of the Self* (New York: International Universities Press, 1977), similarly argued against what he called the "developmental morality" of traditional Freudian ego psychology. He regarded the capacity to sustain and actualize ideals as a central component of mental health.

106　post-Freudian psychoanalytic authors: Among the major figures are D. W. Winnicott, in works such as *The Maturational Process and the Facilitating Environment* (New York: International Universities Press, 1965) and *Playing and Reality* (New York: Basic Books, 1971); Hans Loewald, in works such as *Papers on Psychoanalysis* (New Haven: Yale University Press, 1980); and Heinz Kohut, in works such as *The Restoration of the Self.*

106　Elaine Scarry, *On Beauty and Being Just* (Princeton: Princeton University Press, 1999), p. 48.

106　The quotation from Stuart Hampshire is from his review of Scarry's *On*

Beauty and Being Just: "The Eye of the Beholder," *New York Review of Books,* Nov. 18, 1999, p. 44.

110   construction of the other as an object of desire: Scarry notes that the basic response to an object of beauty is to want to replicate the experience as well as the object. Beautiful persons generate an "impulse toward begetting," which may contribute to explaining their sexual power. In this sense, idealization imparts survival advantages and may have emerged over the course of human evolution partially because of its adaptive function. The idealization generated in sexual passion contributes to the reproduction of the species. We might further speculate that in subsequent stages of a relationship it is more adaptive to regard one's partner more soberly, facilitating cooperation in the hard tasks of living. But again, it would be difficult to assign greater "reality" to one or the other of these perspectives. Is the idealization that draws lovers together based on a repression of their faults and therefore less real than later, less glowing estimations?

111   the sadomasochistic experience of the sexual pervert: S. Bach, "On Sadomasochistic Object Relations," in Gerald Fogle and W. A. Myers, eds., *Perversions and Near-Perversions in Clinical Practice* (New Haven: Yale University Press, 1991), p. 87.

113   As Freud noted long ago: Freud, *On Narcissism: An Introduction* (1914), SE 14: 67–102.

116   Erica Jong, *Fear of Flying* (New York: Signet, 1995), pp. 11, 14.

4. Aggression and the Danger of Desire

124   "war of everyone against everyone": Thomas Hobbes, *Leviathan* (1651; Oxford: Basil Blackwell, 1946, p. 82.

124   Konrad Lorenz, *On Aggression* (New York: Harcourt, Brace and World, 1966).

125   "innate repugnance": Jean Jacques Rousseau, *The First and Second Discourses* (New York: St. Martin's, 1964), p. 130.

125   "War is a relationship": Rousseau, *The Social Contract* (New York: Gateway, 1954), p. 11.

125   "frustration/aggression" hypothesis: John Dollard, Neal Miller, et al., *Frustration and Aggression* (New Haven: Yale University Press, 1939).

125   an innate aggressive drive: Early on, Freud regarded libidinal desire

(along with a concern for self-preservation) as the deep instinctual force motivating people. Aggression played a role, he believed, as a force mobilized in response to direct threats to our survival and as a component of certain facets of sexuality. For example, babies, when their teeth emerge, display oral sadism, occasionally biting the breast that feeds them, but Freud considered their aggression merely a facet of the more global sensual oral pleasure.

Freud's early disciple Alfred Adler thought Freud had not given aggression, the lust for dominance and power, its due by merely positioning it as a component of sexuality. Adler believed aggression was a primary instinctual force in its own right. Freud argued strongly against Adler's heresy, and Adler withdrew from the psychoanalytic world to develop his own theory and treatment for neurosis. However, in what would become a characteristic political strategy in the development of psychoanalytic ideas, Freud eventually absorbed the proposal of his critic without crediting him.

In *Beyond the Pleasure Principle* (1920), Freud introduced the notion of a primary aggressive drive. Aggression, he now argued, was a deep, fundamental instinct, originally independent of both self-preservation and sexuality. In what became known as Freud's "dual instinct theory," sex and aggression were understood to develop in parallel, often combining in a "fusion" in certain kinds of sexual experiences like sadism and masochism. Freud was not just struggling with the fine points of what makes useful psychodynamic theory; he was grappling with our very nature as human beings.

125 dovelike positions emerged: In the 1930s and 1940s the American psychiatrist H. S. Sullivan, one of the ancestors of what came to be known as interpersonal psychoanalysis, wrote about aggression as a "security operation," a defense against anxiety. Heinz Kohut, the developer of contemporary self psychology, wrote about aggression as a self-bolstering, compensatory defense against narcissistic injury.

127 the bonobo: Frans de Waal and Frans Lanting, *Bonobo: The Forgotten Ape* (Berkeley: University of California Press, 1997), p. 154. Consider also the use of aggression by chimpanzees for the establishment and maintenance of power hierarchies and coalitions. Apparently explosive outbreaks of violence, on closer examination, have a much more controlled and purposeful structure: "When two apes come to blows or threaten each other a third ape may decide to enter the conflict and side with one

of them. The result is a coalition of two against one. In many cases the conflict extends still further, and larger coalitions are formed. Because everything happens so quickly, we might imagine that chimpanzees are carried away by the aggression of others and that they join in blindly. Nothing is further from the truth. Chimpanzees never make an uncalculated move." Frans de Waal, *Chimpanzee Politics: Power and Sex among Apes* (Baltimore: John Hopkins University Press, 1989).

130 spiraling physical needs: Freud, *Inhibitions, Symptoms, and Anxiety* (1926), SE 20: 75–175.

130 separation from "attachment" figures: John Bowlby, *Separation: Anxiety and Anger,* vol. 2 of *Attachment and Loss* (New York: Basic Books, 1973).

130 breaks in emotional attunement: Daniel Stern, *The Interpersonal World of the Infant* (New York: Basic Books, 1985).

130 parental anxiety: H. S. Sullivan, *The Interpersonal Theory of Psychiatry* (New York: Norton, 1953).

130 maternal impingement: D. W. Winnicott, *The Maturational Process and the Facilitating Environment* (New York: International Universities Press, 1965).

130 One imaginative developmental theory: Heinrich Racker, *Transference and Countertransference* (New York: International Universities Press, 1968).

130 not only of infantile but of adult reasoning: In *The Body in Pain* (New York: Oxford University Press, 1985), Elaine Scarry points out that "the very word 'pain' has its etymological home in 'poena' or 'punishment' . . . even the elementary act of naming this most interior of events entails an immediate mental somersault out of the body into the external social circumstances that can be pictured as having caused the hurt" (p. 16).

135 Carson McCullers, "The Ballad of the Sad Café," in McCullers, *Collected Stories* (Boston: Houghton Mifflin, 1987), p. 216.

138 a secret form: H. S. Sullivan termed this psychological strategy that allows one to be involved with experiences one cannot directly claim as the security operation of "specious ideals."

139 ". . . the fruits of his crime": Leo Tolstoy, *Anna Karenina* (New York: New American Library, 1961), p. 161.

140 Some theorists of the erotic: Robert J. Stoller, *Observing the Erotic Imagination* (New Haven: Yale University Press, 1992).

140 alluring but unknown strangers: See, e.g., Jean Laplanche, *Life and Death in Psychoanalysis* (Baltimore: John Hopkins University Press, 1976).

5. *Guilt and Self-Pity*

153 from feeling bad to feeling magnanimous: In a subsequent session Ed raised the possibility of reparation accompanied by an acceptance of guilt rather than a defense against guilt. Melanie Klein made the same distinction between what she called "true reparation" and "manic, magic reparation." I take up Klein's illuminating approach to guilt shortly.

154 this nightmare would not be happening: One of the most clinically fruitful contributions of the influential Scottish psychoanalyst W. R. D. Fairbairn was his depiction of what he called the "moral defense."

155 "it is better to be a sinner". Fairbairn, *Repression and the Return of Bad Objects* (New York: Basic Books, 1952), pp. 66–67.

155 responsibility for one's own failings: The experience of shame is closely related to both self-pity and guilt. Shame is a residue of an interpersonal situation of embarrassment and humiliation. One feels ashamed when one has been shamed. And shame is then inevitably transferred into new interpersonal situations, creating either opportunities for growth or constriction and thus further shame.

159 Hans Loewald, "The Waning of the Oedipus Complex," *Journal of the American Psychoanalytic Association* 27 (1979): 751–776.

160 Not all guilt can usefully be reduced: See Martin Buber, "Guilt and Guilt Feelings," in Buber, *Between Man and Man* (New York: Macmillan, 1965), for an existential approach to guilt as authentic, nonneurotic experience along lines similar to the argument I am developing here.

166 "pain at . . . an appearing evil"; "The (believed) goodness": Martha C. Nussbaum, *The Therapy of Desire* (New Jersey: Princeton University Press, 1994), pp. 86–87.

168 Both pathos and guilt: In distinguishing guilt from guiltiness and pathos from pitifulness and self-pity, I am drawing on the work of Leslie Farber, who traced subtle distinctions between aspects of experience we shape through our own agency (will) and uncontrollable aspects of experience we futilely try to muscle under our domination (willfulness): "In willfulness, the life of the will becomes distended, overweening, and obtrusive at the same time that its movements become increasingly separate, sovereign, and distant from other aspects of spirit . . . In willfulness, then, will pursues its own tyrannical course with reckless disdain for what we usually mean by content, unless that content be the will itself." Farber, *Lying, Despair, Jealousy, Envy, Sex, Suicide, Drugs,*

and the Good Life (New York: Basic Books, 1976), p. 50.

170 moving myself to pity: Self-pity is sometimes entangled with issues of shame as well. Here shame is transformed from a consequence of a hurtful interpersonal event, about which one may well feel sadness and pathos, into self-mortification, in which one gets extra mileage out of punishing and exposing oneself, seizing an illusory control by doing to oneself what was traumatically imposed by another.

170 modes of communicating our experiences to others: Patterns of organizing experiences into either pathos or self-pity, guilt or guiltiness, are shaped in original family contexts. Children are taught to experience and rewarded for experiencing self-pity and guiltiness; alternatively, children can be encouraged to allow themselves to contain feelings of pathos and guilt and then to move on.

170 their corrupted twins: I am borrowing this concept of corrupted twins from Emmanuel Ghent's distinction between surrender and its corrupted twin, submission.

171 "blues is fundamentally": Stanley Crouch, *Always in Pursuit: Fresh American Perspectives, 1995–1997* (New York: Pantheon, 1998), p. 108.

6. Control and Commitment in Romantic Love

176 Preconsciousness operates in very much the same way: This account is taken from Daniel Dennett, *Consciousness Explained* (Boston: Little, Brown, 1991), p. 54.

176 we don't in a continuous way: Donnel Stern provides a rich and insightful study of different forms of consciousness in *Unformulated Experience: From Dissociation to Creativity* (New York: Analytic Press, 1997).

181 in some of his case descriptions: Freud, "A Case of Successful Treatment by Hypnotism" (1892), SE 1: 117–128.

181 "metapsychological" theorizing: Freud, *The Unconscious* (1915), SE 14: 161–215.

181 This was the original meaning: Georg Groddeck, *The Book of the It* (New York: Nervous and Mental Disease Pub. Co., 1928).

182 what Erik Erikson termed "identity": In the more recent self psychology, an offshoot of Freudian ego psychology, the self has a core, a nuclear destiny, not the pre-Freudian omnipotent, autonomous will, but a psychic control center of a new sort.

182 inventions of language and cultural images: In some postmodern formulations, what is most authentic about us is the churning fragmentation of unconscious processes that perpetually disperse the false coherences, the illusory subjectivities, the dichotomously gendered, compulsively heterosexual identities that society subjects us to. There is no "doer behind the deed," as Judith Butler puts it in *Gender Trouble: Feminism and the Subversion of Identity* (New York: Routledge, 1990). Lacan repeatedly mocked American ego psychology precisely for attributing to the "self," a narcissistic illusion, qualities of substance and control.

183 "grand narratives": Jean François Lyotard, *The Postmodern Condition* (Minneapolis: University of Minnesota Press, 1984).

185 systematically elaborate their confluence: The two analytic theorists who have worked on this problem most successfully are Leslie Farber and Roy Schafer, and my discussion of these issues draws heavily on their work.

The key features of Farber's approach, drawn from existential philosophy, are these: First, within the complexity of human psychological processes, the will is always present in some form, either in the foreground or in the background. Second, there is a dialectical relationship between the shaping, constructing, agentic action of the will and the various facets of experience being shaped and constructed (both internal bodily processes and external social forces and circumstances). The will can no longer be granted the power of the omnipotent controller of pre-Freudian understanding. Yet any theory that disperses mind into fragmentary motives, omitting an account of the ways of the will, is sorely lacking.

Roy Schafer developed an incisive and systematic critique of traditional psychoanalytic language and theorizing in *A New Language for Psychoanalysis* (New Haven: Yale University Press, 1976) along lines quite similar to Farber's, although drawing on the analytic philosophy of Wittgenstein and Ryle. See Stephen A. Mitchell, *Relational Concepts in Psychoanalysis: An Integration* (Cambridge, Mass.: Harvard University Press, 1988), ch. 7, for a comparison of Farber's and Schafer's approaches.

187 hope for the best: Farber distinguishes between will and what he calls "willfulness." In the latter case, the will claims greater power than it actually has, in a futile attempt to deny the reality of the complex of motives operating at any given time. "Willfulness" is Victorian "willpower," which resurfaced in Sartre's effort to grant consciousness hegemony over

all mental events. Much of what takes place within psychotherapy, in Farber's view, concerns the sorting out of will from willfulness, the increasing discrimination between constructive and self-defeating (willful) exercise of the will.

194 does the naming itself make it into love?: For an incisive and comprehensive exploration of the history of understandings of affect in psychoanalytic ideas, see Charles Spezzano, *Affect in Psychoanalysis: A Clinical Synthesis* (Hillsdale, N.J.: Analytic Press, 1993).

195 reduced to its emotional ingredients: In *Standing in the Spaces* (Hillsdale, N.J.: Analytic Press, 1998), Philip Bromberg explores the distinction between the experience of making a "decision," in which one is more or less adding up pros and cons to come to what feels like an objective, quantitative comparison, and "choice," in which one is making a personal commitment in a situation of some fundamental ambiguity.

197 each offers very particular constraints: Aristotle speaks of this factor as the "material cause" of the eventual product, in contrast to other contributory causal factors like "efficient" causes (the builder), "formal" causes (the building plan), and "final" causes (the purpose for which the structure is built).

198 in a direct causal fashion: Nancy Chodorow, in *The Power of Feelings* (New Haven: Yale University Press, 1999), provides a rich framework for understanding the interaction of various major contributory dimensions of experience—the past, developmental crises, cultural forms and values, and so on—in complex rather than linearly causal terms.

Index

A Note about the Author

Stephen A. Mitchell's untimely death in the year 2000 occurred at the pinnacle of his career as one of the leading figures in relational psychoanalysis. His colleagues at *Psychoanalytic Dialogues* said of him: "Steve's intellectual brilliance and unparalleled personal generosity created the world of relational psychoanalysis. His creative vision altered and expanded the landscape of psychoanalysis but also in related disciplines." Robert Boyers, editor of *Salmagundi*, called Mitchell "one of the most influential American analysts of his generation." The *New York Times* noted: "Dr. Mitchell was known for his lucid and accessible witing about psychoanalytic theory in books that attracted a wide professional and popular audience."

Mitchell studied philosophy as an undergraduate at Yale University, graduating summa cum laude in 1968. He received his doctoral degree in clinical psychology form New York University in 1972, and completed the psychoanalytic training program at the William Alanson White Institute.

In addition to maintaining a private practice in New York City, Mitchell was the founding editor of *Psychoanalytic Dialogues*, which *Newsweek* credited for the recent revival in American psychoanalysis. He was also the first president of the International Association for Relational Psychoanalysis; an adjunct professor and clinical supervisor at New York University's postdoctoral program in psychotherapy and psychoanalysis; and a training and supervising analyst at both New York University and the William Alanson White Institute.